BELIEVE AND ACHIEVE

Overcoming Obstacles to Excel

By ADAM WHEELER

With Craig Sesker

BELIEVE AND ACHIEVE
Overcoming Obstacles to Excel

By Adam Wheeler
With Craig Sesker

Copyright: 2019 Adam Wheeler
Edited by Anne Sesker
Photos by John Sachs, Tony Rotundo, Larry Slater
Published by Kingery Printing
Designed by Angie Hardenbrook
Cost: $20.00

Printed in the United States of America

First Edition

Foreword

By John Bardis
Founder and CEO of MedAssets, Inc., and
2008 U.S. Olympic Team Leader in Greco-Roman wrestling

Adam Wheeler is an American hero, and chances are you have never heard of him. His is a story of a difficult childhood driven by the effects of a broken family, poverty and homelessness.

With the benefit of a relentless drive to succeed, Adam used his remarkable gifts to become the only American Olympic Greco-Roman wrestling medalist in the 2008 Beijing Olympics.

But unlike most who have accomplished the extraordinary in Olympic sport, the path to Beijing, China was anything but conventional for Adam. At 6-foot-3 and 235 pounds, he is hard to miss. For several years, Adam was our second-best wrestler in his weight class on the Olympic ladder. In 2008, he defeated one of our very best American athletes to make the team. For the most part, the Olympic Games were Adam's first major World competition at the Senior level.

To be clear, limited exposure at the World and Olympic level is not a formula for success in the world's oldest and toughest sport. Olympic caliber wrestlers are at the top of the food chain of tough people. And after coaching in the Ultimate Fighting Championships for almost 20 years, my experience supports that conclusion. It was no surprise to learn that in 2014, after very little exposure to the sport, Adam won the No Gi Jiu Jitsu world championship while serving as a member of the Colorado Springs SWAT team.

When you meet Adam Wheeler you will likely be struck by several things, the first of which is an extraordinary physical presence, as well as his intelligent and gentle spirit. While extraordinary genetics are more common among elite athletes, the latter is often harder to find.

I am reminded that while we were training for the Olympics in Beijing our coaches thought it was a good idea to have a friendly soccer match. During one particular run up the pitch, Adam outsprinted the entire team while hurdling over the head of 55-kilogram wrestler Spenser Mango and outrunning teammate T.C. Dantzler, who had run a 4.35-second 40-yard dash as a Division I defensive back for Northern Illinois.

Adam went on to win the bronze medal at the 2008 Olympic Games. But there is much more to his story. There is little about Adam Wheeler's background that would have predicted his remarkable success at the highest levels of his sport.

To be sure, there is more than luck and genetics in the mix when I think about Adam's life and its impact. American history is rich with men and women who made it their mission to put their lives on the line for the greater benefit of others. And there is something about them—a quality each of us wishes we had but so few of us actually possess. Lieutenant General Russel Honore likes to call these heroes our "Sheep Dogs." I remember the General pointing out that a single sheep dog will fight an entire pack of wolves to save a single lamb. There are times when these warriors come home wounded, sometimes without a leg and sometimes they don't make it back at all.

Adam Wheeler's journey is a story of adversity, success and most importantly service to others.

It is a great American story.

CHAPTER 1
California Dreamin'

To say my childhood was tumultuous would be a huge understatement. I overcame more than my share of challenges and obstacles while growing up in southern California.

I was born at Antelope Valley Hospital in Lancaster, California on March 24, 1981. At my first official weigh-in, I tipped the scales at 8 lbs., 6 ounces. I grew up with a younger brother, William, and a younger sister, Leslie. And then my father had three other boys – Mark, Thomas and Paul – from another relationship.

I come from a family of military and veterans, and police officers and firefighters. All four of my brothers and I served in the military. Public service is a big part of my family, starting with my great uncle, George Bailey, who was killed in the Japanese attacks on Pearl Harbor on December 7, 1941.

My grandfather, George's brother, joined the Marine Corps the next day. He wanted to help defend our country during a scary time as the United States entered World War II.

I grew up in a family where the military was highly regarded and we took a great deal of pride in representing our country.

My mother had four brothers – Jim, Joe, John and Jorge – who served in the military. My uncle Terry, from my dad's side, also served. I looked up to all of them for their service.

That sense of pride was something that stuck with me and would carry through my childhood and into adulthood.

I always knew when I was growing up that I was going to work in public service.

It was a path I had wanted to follow.

My hometown of Lancaster is a city of 160,000 people located near the western edge of the Mojave Desert. It is situated 70 miles northeast of Los Angeles and about a two-hour drive from the Pacific Ocean. The temperatures are what you would expect in that part of the country. The weather is nearly ideal. The average summer temperature is around 90 degrees with the average temperature in the winter around 65. You can't beat the weather and the climate in that part of the world. I never owned a winter coat when I was growing up. We never needed one.

Even with the great weather, my life was a struggle from the beginning. When I was 11 months old, near tragedy struck for our family. I wasn't even a year old and I was already in a fight for my life. I spent my first birthday in the hospital. I had a rare blood disease that nearly killed me. The doctors diagnosed me with Hemolytic Uremic Syndrome, a condition that affects the blood and the blood vessels. It results in the destruction of blood platelets (cells involved in clotting), a low red blood cell count (anemia) and kidney failure due to damage to the very small blood vessels of the kidneys.

My parents, Julie and William Wheeler, were understandably freaking out. They were worried I was going to die. While all of this was going on, my mother was about to have another child. She was six months pregnant with my brother. But my mother was there for me. She was at the hospital every day along with my grandmother, Margurite.

I was in really bad shape. My kidneys were failing and I had to be placed on dialysis. My blood was so thin that if anybody touched me, I would bruise. The doctors eventually came to my parents with a grim diagnosis – they had only seen a couple of people live through the disease. I was really sick. And it didn't look good for me.

My mom said it was a "horrible time" and that she wasn't sure I was going to make it.

The doctors were unable to determine exactly how I had contracted the disease, but my blood was infected. Finally, after five weeks in the hospital, I started responding to the treatments. My fortunes remarkably turned around and everyone in my family breathed a huge sigh of relief. Their prayers had been answered.

Apparently, I was a fighter and I was someone who wasn't going to give up. I had survived a near-death experience.

When I was growing up, it looked like I had two belly buttons because of the scar I had from when they cut me open.

The odds were seemingly stacked against me, but I somehow managed to survive. That early scare would serve as a microcosm of my life story as I moved forward.

I really don't have any memories of my parents being together during my childhood. They divorced when I was just three years old. When they split up, I stayed with my mom. My brother and sister also lived with my mother. I didn't see my father very much after that. I really don't have any issues with my dad. I like him and we get along very well. I just never saw him very much. I only saw him for a couple of weeks a year – one or two weeks in the summer and one week over Christmas break as a young kid. He always had presents for us for at Christmas when we went to his house.

Since I've been an adult, I probably talk to my father on the phone once or twice a year. I usually call him and initiate the conversation. Like I said, I get along with my dad. I wouldn't describe our relationship as very close, but I still love him. He only went to one or two of my wrestling matches in high school and he rarely saw me compete. He never saw me wrestle on the Senior level when I competed internationally after high school. At the time, I didn't really think much about him not being there. It wasn't even on my radar that he wasn't there because that's just how it was. That's what I was used to. I don't think my father is a bad person, he's just not very good at communicating.

The absence of my father growing up did take a toll on me, my mother, and my brother and sister. My dad wasn't paying child support and we were on welfare when I was younger. As I would discover, welfare was a type of government support and funding that helps struggling families meet their basic human needs such as food and shelter. And it was something that we needed.

My mom had her hands full. She was trying to raise and support three young kids virtually on her own.

Money was scarce. I didn't really know any differently at first, but as I became older, I started to realize how difficult the situation was for us. Those times were pretty rough on my mother. She did what she could to support us, but it was largely a struggle for her. I do appreciate her efforts – she was in a difficult situation. We knew she cared about us and we knew she loved us. It was not easy for her or for us.

We never seemed to stay in one place for very long in my early days. We often bounced from home to home. There wasn't much stability. That was the life I knew as a child.

A life of transition, mobility and instability.

In my early years, we lived with my grandmother, Jane. She was my mom's mother. My grandfather had passed away when I was really young.

At one point, my mom had a boyfriend and we lived with him for a short period before going back to live with my grandmother again. Her boyfriend was an alcoholic and started becoming abusive toward my mom.

My grandma had a pretty nice house and it was awesome that she gave us a place to stay. My mom was trying to get her life back on track and go back to school. My grandma got lung cancer and my mom took care of her, but eventually my grandmother passed away.

After my grandma died, we were bouncing from house to house again. We lived in at least six different locations. When I was in junior high, we lived in a ghetto area in Lancaster. It was a high-crime area. It wasn't the safest place.

Times became so difficult that we were evicted from our house. The bills weren't being paid and we didn't have anywhere to go. We snuck into a vacant apartment and we crashed there for a brief time. It was a dirty, rundown apartment that we shouldn't have been in. We didn't have any furniture and I had to use my backpack as a pillow. It was a nightmare. It was awful and it was scary.

Times became so tough that I eventually went to live with a buddy of mine, Franky, and his family when I was in junior high. My brother also went and stayed with a friend of his. And my mom and sister went to stay with one of her friends. We were separated from each other for about six months before we eventually reunited and found a place to live. It wasn't that my mom abandoned us – she was trying to support us while facing some personal issues.

We moved around frequently and it became the norm for us. That lifestyle really sucked as a kid. We would move and then have to leave our friends behind. And then we would move into a new neighborhood and we would have to try and make new friends. I know it bothered me, but I didn't think much of it at the time and it didn't affect me as much as it could have. My mom was struggling with a drug addiction and that made it difficult for us as well.

Even though she had her demons to battle, she was always working hard and we always knew she loved us.

One aspect of my life that helped me cope with a rough upbringing was playing sports. It became an escape for me. I poured myself into athletics and it became an important outlet for me.

I was lucky to have an athletic brother. I always had someone to play sports with.

I was an active kid with an abundance of energy, so playing sports was a perfect match for me. One of the benefits of growing up in California is the warm weather. You can play sports outside virtually year-round. And we took full advantage of that. Baseball became my sport of choice and I couldn't get enough of it. I loved to play ball and I could do it almost every day of the year, from sunrise to sunset. There was nothing quite like being out in the bright sunshine playing baseball with my buddies.

One of my first heroes was a baseball player, a kid from my hometown named Sean Douglass. Sean was two years older than me and I grew up playing baseball with him. He was a tremendous player and an outstanding pitcher. He put on a show when he played. You didn't want to take your eyes off Sean Douglass when he stepped on the baseball field. If you did, you might miss something spectacular.

Sean was the kid that we all looked up to and aspired to be like. He was very tall, at 6-foot-6, and he had an incredible arm. Right after he finished high school, Sean was selected in the second round of the major league baseball draft by the Baltimore Orioles.

Sean played five seasons in the major leagues for the Orioles,

BELIEVE AND ACHIEVE

Toronto Blue Jays and Detroit Tigers. He went on to play profession-
ally for a few seasons in Japan.

I grew up with a lot of other kids who excelled in baseball, and
many of them went on to excel in high school and college. One of
those kids was Franky Rosado, who is the most naturally gifted athlete I know.

We had a lot of fun playing baseball in those days. It was competitive and we had kids who played at a very high level. I loved baseball – I still do. I am a die-hard Los Angeles Dodgers fan.

There was one particular day when I wasn't having much fun on
the baseball field. It was a day I will never forget.

I was on third base and one of my teammates hit a ground ball to
one of the infielders. I reacted and made a break for home plate. I
charged down the baseline, pumping my arms and legs as fast as I
could before starting an aggressive slide into the plate. As soon as I
landed on the field, the catcher tagged me before I heard and felt my
leg pop.

My mother also heard it along with the other people sitting next
to her in the stands.

It was such a loud pop that people all the way back in the snack
bar heard it.

I knew immediately that something was wrong.

My right leg was bent in this crazy, awkward position and you
could tell right away that it was broken.

I screamed in horror.

"My leg is broken!" I yelled. "My leg is broken!"

I don't remember exactly how I knew that.

I just knew.

And I was in excruciating pain.

My coach sprinted onto the field and my mom rushed down from
her seat in the stands.

Making matters worse was that I didn't even score on the play.
My body didn't move when I hit the ground. I didn't slide at all and
the catcher tagged me out.

A short time later, paramedics arrived at the field and it took
them a while before they could transport me to the hospital.

It took them about 45 minutes to straighten my leg.

I wasn't in shock, but I was kind of in a fog. I obviously remember my leg really hurting.

It was pretty scary and traumatic for someone my age.

It was the first bone I had ever broken.

I certainly got my money's worth on that one.

I had landed awkwardly when I had completed my slide into home. I broke my femur bone. I had suffered a compound fracture. The lower portion of my femur bone got pushed up over the upper portion. It was a gruesome injury.

And I was faced with a very long road to recovery.

That was rough for an 11-year-old boy to endure. I couldn't play baseball, and I couldn't run around and play with my friends. Not to mention the fact that it was difficult just to get around the house while not being able to function normally.

After the injury, I was in traction at the hospital for two weeks. The doctors inserted pins into my knees and put weights on it to help pull my bones back into the right place.

I was in a full body cast for four months. That was really hard on me. It seemed like an eternity. It was horrible.

Looking back, I realize how hard this was on my mother. She had to take care of me day and night, including helping me go to the bathroom since I was unable to get out of my bed without assistance.

Finally, I was placed in a smaller leg cast before I was able to resume full activity.

I underwent intensive physical therapy. It was a long process. The therapy was painful and I hated it. But I had to do it.

It was the next season before I was able to play baseball again. It had been a full year since my injury. That was difficult.

I was not a happy camper during that time. It was tough on me.

Once I got out of the smaller cast, I immediately noticed the difference in my mobility. I wasn't quite the same as I was before my injury. Not even close.

I had gained a significant amount of weight. I was already a big kid, but then I packed on even more weight because of inactivity. What little muscle tone I had before the injury was pretty much gone.

BELIEVE AND ACHIEVE

It had atrophied from not being active for six months. I had been pretty athletic before my injury, but I had lost a lot of my mobility and athleticism. I was still one of the better baseball players in our area, but I couldn't run as fast or move as well. That was a significant adjustment for me and it was a little frustrating at times.

Before the injury, I wasn't the fastest kid but I was one of the fastest.

After the injury, I was the slowest kid.

To this day, my right leg is a little bit shorter than my left leg.

I still walk with a little bit of a limp from that injury.

It took me a long time to be able to run full speed again.

The following baseball season, I came back strong. I led the league in home runs. I wasn't able to run as fast as I could before the injury and that was something I had to adapt to. It took a long time to recover from the broken leg. I started playing baseball when I was five years old and it was a sport that I excelled in. It was the first organized sport I played. The positions I played were first base, third base, pitcher and catcher. I hit with some power. I just loved to play ball, and it's what most kids did while growing up in California. I played baseball through my freshman year of high school.

No matter what was going on or how much we were struggling with money or trying to make ends meet, my mom never missed one of my sporting events. I could always look up in the stands and count on her being there. She was always supportive and wanted the best for us. She was my No. 1 fan. When we got older, we started acting up and making things tougher for her. We were immature and disobedient. And that wasn't fair to her. She was always nice to us. She was trying to make the best of a difficult and trying situation.

Life was never easy for us. We dealt with more than our fair share of hardships. There was one year that was particularly rough on us around the holidays. We didn't celebrate Christmas at our house because there was no money. I was in seventh grade and my mom was struggling. She couldn't afford to buy us anything. We didn't get any Christmas presents. We didn't say anything about it because we understood the magnitude of the situation. It was a tough time.

We were living in a small house in Lancaster. I was afraid to walk outside at night because it was a really rough area that we lived in. My mother was working two jobs to try and support our family. There were times we didn't have much food in the house. And there were times we didn't have much supervision at night because my mom was working.

A lot of days she would come home between jobs and we would see her for just a short time. And then she was off to her other job. It wasn't an ideal situation, but it was the one that we were in.

There are several instances that illustrate how rough that area of Lancaster was.

When I was in junior high, I was walking home from school one day with some kids who lived by us. Another group of kids were approaching and they walked up to us. One guy in their group pulled a knife out and tried to stab one of the kids in our group. It was pretty scary. We all took off running.

Another time, we were at a party when I was in junior high. I got talked into fighting this other seventh-grader. Then an older guy pulled out a gun and pointed it at my head. He said, "Why are you wearing a green shirt?" Apparently, the color of the shirt I was wearing matched the colors of one of their rival gangs. He eventually put the gun away when he realized I wasn't in a gang. I couldn't believe that happened. It scared the hell out of me and it obviously shook me up a little bit. That was crazy, but unfortunately a lot of those kinds of things were going on in our neighborhood. I never felt totally safe living there, that's for sure.

After all of the moving around, there was finally some stability when I was in high school. We lived in the same house for all four years that I was in high school. My mom found a good job and we finally had some stability.

It wasn't the nicest area of town, but it was a home. During the time we were there, I met some of my best friends who I still talk to now. It was a blue-collar area, much nicer than where we had lived before. This neighborhood was still pretty rough at times.

There were two drive-by shootings a few houses down from us. They were gang-related shootings. I didn't hear the gunfire, but I heard the sirens and saw the police cars flying by our house to where a shooting had occurred. I went outside and then walked down the street and saw the guy who had been shot. It was pretty surreal. He was screaming at the police. He ended up being OK, but it was a little scary. The guy who had been shot was actually a kid that I knew and played with. He was a year older than me. That hit home. We realized just how dangerous the neighborhood was.

Baseball was my sport, but I decided to give another sport a try. I started wrestling my freshman year in high school. Honestly, I had no idea about wrestling. All I knew about it was from a wrestling scene that I saw from one of my favorite TV shows, "Saved by the Bell." I saw actor Mario Lopez portraying a wrestler on the show. I didn't know it at the time, but Lopez had actually placed at the state tournament as a high school wrestler in California. I didn't think the TV scene he was in about wrestling was super cool or anything. It was just the only exposure that I had to wrestling. I saw a flyer at my school about wrestling and I thought that it was something I wanted to try. I told my mom about it when I got home.

"I'm thinking about trying out for the wrestling team," I said.

"Do you know what they have to wear?" she responded matter-of-factly while shaking her head.

I was kind of a chubby kid and my mom told me about the skin-tight, spandex singlets that the wrestlers wore to compete in. Even though I was a chubby kid, the singlet was fine. I didn't mind wearing it.

I knew if I was going to wrestle, I wanted to have the proper equipment. So I had to get a pair of wrestling shoes. My mom couldn't afford wrestling shoes, so I went door-to-door asking people in our neighborhood if I could mow their lawns to earn money. I had earned $15 before a family friend of ours, Scott Raanes, offered to buy me a pair of shoes. Scott was like an uncle to me and I really appreciate his generosity. My first pair of wrestling shoes were Nike Greco. I wore them for two seasons. My new shoes were black with a white Nike swoosh. They probably weren't the most expensive wrestling shoes, but I didn't care. I appreciated having shoes that I could wrestle in.

I had the proper equipment, but I had a rude introduction to the sport of wrestling. I was a horrible wrestler in the beginning. I was awful, just awful. I got a late start into the sport and many of the kids my age had already been wrestling for a number of years. They already knew a lot of the moves and techniques.

I was a first-time wrestler as a freshman in high school and it showed. I went 1-15 while wrestling for the freshman team at Lancaster High School. During my first practice, I remember the coaches wanted to check our level of conditioning. I had no idea how to wrestle and no idea how to train. We had to run one mile around the track at our school. Four laps around the track equaled one mile. I knew I wasn't in the best shape, but I had no idea how bad it was until I started running. I had to stop before we finished the first lap because I was out of breath. It was embarrassing and a little humiliating. I was overweight and out of shape, and that was exposed in my first workout.

I had no mental toughness, a huge aspect of being a good wrestler. I had to walk the next three laps just to finish the mile. It wasn't pretty.

Going into my first tournament as a high school freshman, we boarded a bus to travel to the event. I was so nervous the whole drive there. I wasn't afraid to lose because I didn't know any better. I was afraid of being hurt by the kids who were stronger and more experienced. I had no confidence.

I lost every single match that year except for one. I was lucky in the one match that I won that year. A guy shot in and I caught him with a move called a cow-catcher and I pinned him. It was toward the end of the season. It was early in the match. He was another freshman who looked like he was new to wrestling. He took a sloppy shot and I grabbed his chin and I was able to launch him to his back. I can still picture that match almost 25 years later. It was a sense of accomplishment to win. That was important for me. Winning a match and having a small taste of success was huge. If I had lost every match that season, I may not have come back and wrestled the next season. Winning that match was one of the main reasons I stuck with it.

There was some kind of internal drive in me where I wanted to get stronger and I wanted to get better. I obviously knew I had plenty of room for improvement.

I wrestled in the 189-pound weight class as a freshman after starting out the season weighing 200 pounds. I couldn't do one legitimate pushup at the start of the year. Not one. I know that's hard to believe, but it absolutely is true.

I was around 5-foot-8 and I was a chubby kid who wasn't very strong. During Christmas break, I started doing pushups. I would do one or two good pushups multiple times a day and then try to build on that. When I returned to school after Christmas break, one of my coaches complimented me because I could do five or six good pushups in a row. That still wasn't very many, but it was an improvement.

I was determined to get in shape. I would finish wrestling practice after school, and then I would go home and eat dinner before doing another workout. I bought my own gym membership for $16 a month –

I mowed lawns to pay for it. I worked out at a place called Family Fitness – it is now a 24-Hour Fitness. I went to the gym in the evenings after dinner and started lifting weights. I was determined to improve. I was also lucky enough to have a neighbor, Aaron Wintterle, who was a year older than me. He was a lot stronger and more athletic than me. We became best friends and workout partners for the remainder of high school.

Toward the end of my freshman year, one of our assistant wrestling coaches was telling some of my teammates that they could go to wrestling camps during the summer so they could learn and improve.

I approached the coach and I asked him about attending a camp. He stopped me in my tracks.

"Adam, I don't think you're ready for a camp," the coach told me.

Those words really motivated me. When people thought I couldn't do something, that really pushed me and drove me. That coach was probably right because I wasn't very advanced with my skill set. But I was going to keep working hard so I could improve.

My mom was dumbfounded by what I was doing. She couldn't quite figure out why I was trying to wrestle and trying a new sport. I had played baseball for years and she knew that I was a pretty good baseball player. She also could see that I wasn't having much success in wrestling.

Overcoming Obstacles to Excel

"Why don't you just stick with baseball?" she asked.

There was just something about wrestling that really appealed to me and really drew me to the sport. Maybe it was because the sport was so challenging. And maybe it was because I could see the harder that I worked the better I became.

I'm not sure what exactly I was thinking as a 15-year-old kid who had just started high school, but I know I was determined to improve. And I wasn't about to quit.

I was looking for any kind of an edge I could get. I bought body-building magazines and tried to do the workouts they were doing. Of course, at the time I had no idea those guys were on steroids and that was why many of them looked the way they did.

During my freshman year, I didn't play high school baseball in the spring. I was struggling academically. I ended up being ineligible to play for the high school team. My grades slipped at the end of my first year. I failed a math class and I fell behind academically.

I came back for my sophomore year at Lancaster High with much more confidence than I had the year before. I had grown a couple of inches to 5-foot-10 and I was much-improved in wrestling. Unfortunately, I hadn't improved much in the classroom. The progress reports came out and my grades were bad. I was kicked off the wrestling team for grades. My record was 15-15 when that happened. I was still voted the most improved wrestler on the team and I received an award for it. I had worked hard in the summer between my freshman and sophomore year, lifting weights and doing cardio workouts. I really got myself in shape. But I stopped going to school during my sophomore year and started smoking pot with my friends. I was partying and drinking, and staying out too late. I was sneaking out of the house late at night to hang out with my friends. I was definitely headed down the wrong path.

My mom would try to wake me up for school and I wouldn't get up. I had become very disobedient. I ended up dropping out of Lancaster High School. My life was spiraling out of control. I enrolled at Desert Wind, a school where all of the kids that got in trouble went. I was only at that school for a short time. I thought it would be easier there, but I hated it. It wasn't a good place to be.

BELIEVE AND ACHIEVE

My mother was working two jobs while I was in high school, so we were home alone quite a bit. And we had plenty of opportunities to land in trouble.

Before I left Lancaster High late in my sophomore year, I ran into my wrestling coach.

"Hey Coach, I'm not going to be able to wrestle for you anymore," I told him.

I was ineligible and I was dropping out of that school.

At that point, my wrestling coach took me under his wing.

John Eisel was his name and I'm so blessed I ran into him that day at school.

My life was on a downward spiral and he stepped in and basically saved my life. He talked to the school and helped get me back into Lancaster High as a junior. This wasn't an easy task for him. He had to go through many steps for me to be able to go back. One step in the process was that I had to speak to a school psychologist, who wrote a letter of recommendation for me.

I had earned no credits from any of my classes during my sophomore year, so I was way behind. Coach Eisel informed me that I wouldn't be allowed to play sports the first semester of my junior year, but by the time wrestling started I would be eligible if I maintained my grades. My coach was on me to make sure I did my school work. I took extra classes my junior and senior year to catch up on credits. I took college classes four nights a week, did independent study and went to summer school.

Coach Eisel picked me up at 5 a.m. on Saturdays for a hike or a workout. And then he would take me to church on Sunday mornings. I didn't have any church clothes, so he bought me clothes to wear. I wore those same clothes to church for the next two years. I never felt comfortable going to church, but I went almost every Sunday.

Coach Eisel would take me to the track to do running workouts. I would always have to run for at least 25 minutes. We would do extra workouts and he would do all of them with me. Coach Eisel put a lot of time and effort into me. I'm not sure what he saw in me, but I'm really glad that he took such an interest in helping me follow the right path. He taught me to respect people and be disciplined. He provided me with the guidance and direction that I so badly needed. He was a coach, a mentor, a role model and a father figure for me. He totally turned my life around. He had a huge impact on me. I can't thank him enough for what he did for me.

During my junior year, my mentality had switched. I was working out twice a day and I became very serious about wrestling. I grew into my body and I was learning new techniques. I had become a little bit taller and I was now 6-foot-1 before growing to 6-3 my senior year.

I made a huge jump on the wrestling mat as well. I compiled a 37-7 record on varsity as a junior and I became the first league champion in the history of Lancaster High School.

Nobody was telling me I wasn't good enough to go to a wrestling camp in the summer anymore. Now I was ready to go to one of the elite camps. My mom couldn't afford it, but she applied for a grant for J Robinson's camp. The J Robinson Intensive Camps were recognized as the toughest and best camps in the country for high school wrestlers. J Robinson was a long-time assistant coach under the legendary Dan Gable at the University of Iowa before winning three NCAA championships as the head coach at Minnesota. My request for a grant to the camp was approved and I headed to northern California for the camp between my junior and senior year of high school. They called it an intensive camp and it was every bit of that. It was two weeks of hell and I definitely hated it at times. They pushed us to the limits and the idea was to train us the way they would train their elite college athletes.

All-American Brandon Eggum of Minnesota was in college at that time and he was helping as one of the coaches. He went on to win a World silver medal and is now the head coach at Minnesota. I received a really rude awakening at that camp. There was a guy there named Andy Varner, a very tough wrestler from Bakersfield, California. He weighed 170 pounds and I was around 215 pounds. Guys were talking about how good Varner was and I made a comment to them that nobody who weighed 170 pounds was going to beat me. I ended up regretting those words.

Andy Varner came up to me at practice and looked me straight in the eyes.

"Hey, I heard nobody's that 170 pounds could beat you," Varner said.

"Yeah, I don't think they could," I responded.

That was a bad mistake. I probably should've kept my mouth shut. Andy Varner proceeded to beat the living crap out of me for the next two hours at practice. He was double-legging me and just destroying me. I felt like I couldn't breathe. Andy went on to wrestle at the Division I level in college and his cousin, Jake, would win an Olympic gold medal for the U.S. in wrestling in 2012. I learned a pretty valuable lesson that day from Andy Varner. You're never quite as good as you think you are. Looking back, I appreciate that lesson.

The intensive camp was really tough, grueling and demanding. We did three workouts a day and we were exhausted when we climbed into bed every night. It was very, very intense. I didn't learn a ton of new techniques at that camp, but I built some confidence and I definitely improved my mental toughness after being put through some of the most grueling workouts I had ever done.

On the last day of the camp, we were asked to complete a 12-mile run. It wasn't easy, but I was able to finish it. Not bad for a guy who weighed 215 pounds. I had come a long way since being unable to run one lap around the track as a high school freshman. I was able to meet and learn from all of the college wrestlers who worked with us at the camp. And I had a chance to wrestle against some tough opponents. They gave us a shirt at the end of the camp that had the words, "I DID IT" prominently displayed on the front. It was definitely an accomplishment and a source of pride for me to make it through a difficult two weeks. It definitely made a difference for me and made me a better wrestler.

Believe it or not, my mental toughness would be put to an even tougher test during that same summer. Coach Eisel would take me on these hikes on Saturdays. We would hike for an hour or two, and it was a great workout for us. It also was a time when he would provide me with knowledge about other aspects of life and talk to me about being a man.

But on this particular day, it was different. It was 100 degrees outside. We were near the Mojave Desert – it was a blazing hot day and the heat was stifling. We saw a rattlesnake early in the hike and we eventually got away from it. It ended up being a grueling, excruciating hike. It was a little farther than my coach had expected and what we planned for with our water supply. We ran out of water 10 miles into the hike. It ended up being a 25-mile hike in the desert, roughly the equivalent of a 26.2-mile marathon road race. However, this marathon was up and down huge hills and mountains way out in the desert heat.

After about 15 miles, we literally thought we were going to die. We were exhausted and dehydrated with no end to the hike in sight. We were only going about 100 or 200 yards at a time before we had to stop and take a break. We were lucky if we could find a small piece of shade.

It was crazy. I was looking for some shade where I could just lie down and rest. I didn't want to take another step. We were going up and down these hills, and it was incredibly difficult. That was a time where my mindset switched. We basically hiked a marathon in the blazing California sun. It was brutal and we were struggling. We had to really become mentally strong and realize we had to keep pushing. We literally could've died that day. It's one of the hardest things I have ever done physically and mentally. I still give my coach a hard time for almost killing us that day. He thought it was 12 miles and it ended up being twice that far.

We finally saw my coach's truck, parked at the end of the trail. That definitely was encouraging, but it still took us another two hours to get to it. It was almost like a mirage because it felt like we weren't getting any closer. That was something that really built my mental toughness. After accomplishing that, I felt like I could do anything and take on any challenge.

I was so tired and I wanted to quit. It was that bad. We had blisters on our feet. I kept trying to drink out of the water bottle to just get one drop. The bottle had been out of water for hours, but I kept trying to drink out of it. I don't know for sure how long it took us to complete the hike. We left my house early in the morning and we didn't get back home until dark. We were pretty quiet at times during that hike and afraid of what was going to happen. Neither one of wanted to acknowledge that by saying anything. We were very fortunate something bad didn't happen to us.

It had been a wild, wacky and crazy summer, complete with experiencing the grueling J Robinson Intensive Camp followed by a near-death experience in oppressive heat in the California mountains. Those experiences weren't exactly pleasant, but they had definitely made me stronger. I was in the best shape of my life. I was ready to conquer just about any obstacles that came my way.

My senior year of high school was approaching, and I was ready for my best wrestling season yet. I had come a long way from being a guy who couldn't even run one lap around the track and couldn't do one pushup.

The transformation I made physically and mentally from my freshman year to my senior year was pretty remarkable when I think back on it now. I was in terrible shape when I first started wrestling.

It definitely took some time, but I learned I could push myself to limits that I never could have imagined. And that served me well as I continued to make improvements and gains on the wrestling mat.

I was excited for the wrestling season to start. I had worked really hard over the summer. I was bigger and stronger, and I was ready to take on the world. I was finally confident in my abilities. I was coming off a good junior season and I felt like I was ready to win a California state title.

My goal was to win a championship. My grades were good. My relationships with my family were good. All aspects of my life were on track.

The wrestling season started and I was on a roll. I won the first 37 matches my senior season at 215 pounds.

I was undefeated and my confidence level was as high as it had ever been.

In my 38th match of the season, I was winning and looking for a fall. I attempted a far-side cradle on a kid. I jumped across my opponent and tried a risky move by going across my own back to turn him. He posted his hand on the mat to stop my momentum and reversed me to my back.

Later in the match, I tried the same move with a cradle and it backfired again. I ended up losing by two points. I didn't wrestle smart and made some mistakes. I felt like my opponent didn't beat me. I had defeated myself by taking an unnecessary gamble.

That loss haunted me. My dream of an undefeated season was over. I was upset. As I came off the mat, one of our assistant coaches came up to me.

"Are you all right, Adam?" he said.

I shook my head in frustration.

"Yeah, I'm all right."

I was pissed off that I lost and I had finished second at that tournament. I did learn from it, I was just upset that I lost.

I was still super confident and I felt like I could beat anybody.

I bounced back to win my next seven matches before running into another tough opponent. I trailed by a point late in the match against a strong kid and I was unable to score a takedown. I was 44-2 after that loss.

I knew I would have an opportunity to wrestle the kid again at the Masters tournament and I would beat him in the rematch.

My routine had become altered during my training for the Masters event. I was the only one from my team who had qualified for the Masters meet. My practices over those two weeks consisted of wrestling with my coaches and running.

I give huge credit to two of my coaches, Steve Radford and Mike Henery, for doing everything they could to help me. None of my teammates were there to train with me.

I didn't do a very good job of preparing for the Masters tournament.

And it cost me.

I lost my first match at the Masters. The kid who beat me wasn't as good as I was. Things just weren't clicking for me. I lost by a point. I wasn't in it mentally for some reason and I didn't perform to my capability. There were no excuses. It was my fault that I lost and I accept full blame for that performance.

It was devastating, and it really hurt. I felt like I was good enough to win a state title.

BELIEVE AND ACHIEVE

That kid who beat me had to win his next match or I was out. He lost and I was done.

My high school wrestling career was over.

I believed at that time there was a really good chance that was going to be the last match I was ever going to wrestle. I wasn't getting any college scholarship offers even though I had a combined record of 81-10 in my last two years of high school.

But I fell short of qualifying for the state tournament and I am sure that worked against me.

I likely was going into the military.

I wanted to keep wrestling, a sport I had made huge improvements in, but I wasn't sure how I could make that happen.

I planned on joining the U.S. Marine Corps. My best friend, Aaron, and I were going to join together. A lot of my family was in the Marines and that was considered the toughest branch of the military. I had the mentality through wrestling that I wanted to challenge myself and be a Marine.

But that all changed when another friend of mine, Cody Camou, talked to me about going to see the U.S. Coast Guard recruiter with him. They showed me a cool video and talked to me about all of the benefits of joining. They said I could always live by the beach. I was sold.

They sent me the paperwork and I immediately signed it. I was a pretty good swimmer and I wanted to be a rescue swimmer for the Coast Guard. I was a lifeguard when I was in high school.

I also was told by the recruiter that there was a possibility I could wrestle while I was in the military. That really appealed to me.

It's difficult to quantify just how far I progressed in those years. I became a totally different person. I went from a high school dropout who was smoking pot and drinking to someone who had become driven and disciplined.

I was headed down a path of self-destruction and thankfully I had a caring and compassionate coach who stepped in and saved my life. I would hate to think of where I might have ended up if he hadn't helped me.

John Eisel had one of the biggest impacts of anyone in my life.

Overcoming Obstacles to Excel

He definitely came into my life at the most opportune time.
John straightened me out.
He got me back on the wrestling mat and back on track.
And I'm incredibly thankful for that. He saved my life.

CHAPTER 2
Full Steam Ahead

I was accepted into the United States Coast Guard and I reported for the start of boot camp in Cape May, New Jersey, in July 1999. I was 18 years old and I had just graduated from high school.

Graduation was a huge relief for me because of all the extra work I had to do to graduate with my class.

Between the extra work and my wrestling, I had a new mindset moving forward.

I thought boot camp was going to be really difficult with all of the physical activity and challenges that they would make us endure.

There were definitely parts of boot camp that were challenging, but physically wasn't as hard as I thought it would be.

It was nowhere near as difficult as training for wrestling. I remember other recruits were sore and quitting on their pushups, and I thought they were a little weak for not being able to do them.

But looking back, I realize that my mindset was not like most people and the struggle might have been new for some of them.

I knew first-hand what they were going through.

I had come a long way from my early struggles with pushups as a high school freshman.

My experience in wrestling changed all of that for me, physically and mentally.

Nobody works harder than wrestlers. I was already in excellent shape going into boot camp. Marching around and doing pushups wasn't that physically demanding for me. Especially after all of the training that I had done in wrestling.

One big adjustment that I encountered when I went to boot camp was the schedule. Prior to boot camp, I appreciated my sleep.

In boot camp, we would go to bed every night at 10 p.m., if we were lucky. Then in the middle of the night we were required to wake up for an hour to conduct "night watch." After our watch, we could go back to sleep, if possible. But then we had to wake back up around 4:30 in the morning.

That doesn't sound so bad, but doing it for eight weeks became mentally draining.

I was battling sleep deprivation. That was a major adjustment for me.

As you might expect, we were in the water a lot during boot camp. We had swimming requirements to be in the Coast Guard. The swimming part was pretty easy for me. As a kid, I was on swim teams in the summer and as a teenager I was a lifeguard.

One of the reasons that I chose to go into the Coast Guard was because they had informed me that I would have an opportunity to compete for the Navy Wrestling Team. That was something that caught my attention and it was something I was definitely interested in pursuing.

I also wanted to be a helicopter rescue swimmer, considered one of the most difficult jobs in the Coast Guard. I have always been motivated by challenging myself physically.

I arrived at my first unit in Hilo, Hawaii, on Coast Guard Cutter Kiska.

In boot camp, they asked us to list four locations where we would like to my stationed. Hawaii was my third choice. My first two locations were in my home state of California. My fourth choice was in the state of Washington.

I chose California because I was still very young and I wanted to be close to home.

But Hawaii was the next best option.

I was really happy that I was stationed in Hawaii. I loved it there. It was a beautiful place and I am thankful I ended up there.

I wasn't stationed in one of the big areas where people typically go on vacation, like Honolulu or Maui.

Hilo is on the big island and it was a little more desolate than I expected. And it rained quite a bit. It didn't have the crystal blue water the other places in Hawaii had.

It was still beautiful in Hilo. It was green, lush and had breathtaking views. I was excited when I got there.

While stationed in Hawaii, I was able to visit all of the islands. That included a four-month stay on the island of Oahu. We were very close to Honolulu and I enjoyed all of the popular tourist locations.

While in Oahu, I stayed in an apartment with my good friend, Paul. We were there for "Dry Dock," to conduct maintenance on our boat. We worked very long days. We would take the boat out of the water so we could do a total overhaul of all the maintenance needs.

While in Oahu, I lived right next door to a 24-Hour Fitness. I worked out every day and I was able to go surfing on the weekends. I was young and single, and I loved it. I was able to hang out with my buddies and enjoy the nightlife.

Honolulu truly is an amazing place and we took advantage of it.

I made a lot of really good friends when I was in Hawaii. We had some good times there, but I was still focused on working out and staying in shape for wrestling.

When I was new to my unit, I went in and approached my boss, Kai Christensen.

I had only been there for a couple of weeks, so I was a little intimidated.

"The recruiting office in California had said I could wrestle for the Navy team and I wanted to see if that was still a possibility," I asked.

"I'm sorry, I have no idea how it works," Kai told me.

That was crushing news.

I had been told I would have an opportunity to wrestle.

That obviously was not the news I was hoping to hear.

"Recruiters lie a lot to get guys in the military," Kai said. "If what you're saying is true, I don't know if the commander would let you go wrestle because we need you here as part of the staff."

I was disappointed and surprised to hear that, but I had made a commitment to the Coast Guard. I was 18 years old and I was living in Hawaii. And I was enjoying what I was doing while working in one of the most beautiful places on the planet.

Luckily for me, Kai did some research and found out that I could try out for the Navy wrestling team. Before he told me, he had it approved.

If Kai hadn't looked into it, I may have been done with wrestling and would have focused on my career in the Coast Guard.

I am so grateful to Kai for checking on that.

If it wasn't for wrestling, I wouldn't have gone to college and I wouldn't have met my wife. I wouldn't have been able to travel around the world and wrestle in so many prestigious events.

Wrestling opened so many doors for me. It's crazy the path that the sport took me on. I'm very grateful for that.

My next step was to contact the coach of the Navy wrestling team. I was given a phone number and told to place a call to a coach named Rob Hermann. I filled out my application and I called him.

"We have four tryouts every year at different Navy bases," Coach Hermann said matter-of-factly.

I was concerned because being in Hawaii meant I would be unable to attend one of the tryouts.

A couple of weeks later, Coach Hermann contacted me and said they needed some big guys to wrestle.

He liked my high school resume and he knew I was a big guy. I was fortunate because very few upper-weight wrestlers tried out that year.

About a month later, the Navy flew me to Pensacola, Florida. I met Rob for the first time and I learned that he was the Olympic Greco-Roman coach for the 1996 Olympic Games in Atlanta.

I was definitely intimidated and felt very fortunate to be working with such a high-caliber coach.

I went through a three-month training camp with the Navy team. I was thinking I was going to wrestle freestyle because that was a style that I had wrestled in during high school. But Rob also asked me to try Greco-Roman wrestling. There weren't very many tough guys on the Navy team at the 213-pound weight class, so he wanted me to try both styles. Rob's coaching specialty was in Greco.

Greco-Roman is a style consisting of upper-body wrestling where you can't attack your opponent's legs. You can score with an array of lifts and throws.

The elite Greco guys were proficient at launching opponents with spectacular, high-amplitude moves where you could score big points and put on a show for the fans.

At the time, I had very little interest in Greco-Roman wrestling because it was a style that I wasn't familiar with. And quite honestly, I was a little afraid to be thrown.

After the training camp, there was a tryout to see who would represent the Navy team at the Armed Forces Championships.

I won in Greco-Roman and freestyle at the all-Navy wrestle-offs and that was a huge turning point for me. I made the Navy team and I was able to compete in the Armed Forces Championships in 2000. It was one of the best events I had ever wrestled in.

The United States had a large group of strong Greco wrestlers who were in the military. Standout heavyweight Dremiel Byers, who went on to win a World title and make two Olympic teams, was among the wrestlers. Byers was a member of the U.S. Army's World Class Athlete Program.

My first match at my first Armed Forces tournament was against this monster named Josh Hall, who wrestled for the Army. He was a big, strong, powerful guy and he easily defeated me by a technical fall.

I wrestled Dan Hicks of the Marines Corps in the next match. He was ranked No. 2 in the country. He kicked my butt before pinning me. It was a rude awakening.

I was fresh out of high school and wrestling full-grown men in their 20s and 30s who had extensive experience wrestling internationally.

I was a teenager with no experience on the Senior level. The last matches I had wrestled were against high school competition.

I wrestled an Air Force guy in my third and final Greco-Roman match of the day. He snapped me down with a front headlock, but I came back and I high-dived him with a body lock to his back. I locked my arms tightly around his waist and pinned him.

BELIEVE AND ACHIEVE

It was an awesome feeling when the referee raised my arm to signify that I had won the match.

I had earned my first victory on the Senior level.

I was excited to accomplish that in my first tournament on that level.

My teammate, Steven Mays, congratulated me after the match. I really felt like I accomplished something. Steve was a great wrestler and a great guy. He made the U.S. Olympic Team in Greco in 2000. He was elected captain of the squad by his teammates.

I had never seen anyone work as hard as Steve. He was a true leader for our young Navy team.

After winning my first Senior-level bout, I came back to wrestle in the freestyle portion of the Armed Forces Championships the next day.

I liked freestyle better than Greco, so I figured I might fare better in freestyle.

But that didn't happen.

My first match was against Mike Van Arsdale of the Army. He was really good and I knew I would have my hands full when I stepped on the mat to face him. Mike was an NCAA champion who went on to excel in the Ultimate Fighting Championships. I was completely out of my league and out of my element when I wrestled Mike Van Arsdale. I thought I was going to wrestle freestyle at that time, but I really struggled in that tournament. I was nowhere near the level of the guys I was facing in freestyle.

In my defense, I was just 18 years old. I wasn't even a year out of high school, and I was out there on the mat wrestling against grown men with beards and chiseled physiques. I was 6-foot-3 and 215 pounds, but I hadn't filled out physically yet.

Wrestling in my first Armed Forces Championships was eye-opening. And it motivated me and inspired me. It convinced me that I wanted to keep wrestling.

Being able to win a match was huge for my psyche. That small taste of success was enough to keep me motivated and hungry to improve and evolve.

Coach Hermann knew I wasn't quite ready to compete at the

U.S. Nationals that year, and he was right. He sent me back to my command in Hawaii and I began preparing for the following year's Armed Forces wrestling event.

Right before I left, I told my teammates that I would come back the strongest 213-pounder in the country.

They didn't realize how serious I was, but that was my mission.

When I returned to my post in Hawaii, I knew what I needed to do. I needed to become bigger and stronger because those Senior-level guys were so physical. I found a high school in Hawaii that I could train at in wrestling.

One of my buddies from work that I trained with convinced me to start doing cardio workouts with him in the morning. We would do a three-mile run or do a swimming workout. We could swim into work and we did that on occasion.

Every day in the evening, we lifted weights.

On the weekends, we would surf. That was our cross-training workout. I had never surfed before. The guys I went with would surf and I would paddle around on my board.

I would try to get up on the board, but it wasn't pretty. Every once in a while, I would ride a wave but that's about it. I loved being in the water. There is something special about being out in the ocean and having that camaraderie with your buddies. I built friendships with guys I am still in contact with.

Hawaii is one of the most beautiful places in the world and the weather there is great year-round. I'm so grateful that the Coast Guard stationed me there. I really enjoyed my time in Hawaii. It was awesome.

I worked in search and rescue, and law enforcement my first two years in the Coast Guard. I gave up on becoming a helicopter rescue swimmer because the wait for school was around four years. I didn't mind because I was still able to be a rescue swimmer for my boat and I was able to wrestle.

In my first job in the Coast Guard, we had a rescue swimmer crew that worked at the Ironman Triathlon in Kona. The Ironman is considered the world's most challenging endurance event. It was really awesome seeing these people push themselves to their limits in a grueling competition that includes swimming 2.4 miles, cycling 112 miles and running a 26.2-mile marathon without taking a break. It was inspiring to watch these athletes compete. That is the ultimate endurance test for your mind and body. These are the most hard-core and dedicated athletes you will ever see.

Wrestlers are some of the most dedicated and hard-working athletes in any sport, but seeing the triathletes compete was quite an experience. They impressed me.

After that first Armed Forces tournament I was determined to become an elite wrestler.

I was invited back to wrestle with the Navy team the next year in 2001. I had made drastic improvements and Coach Hermann noticed that.

I wrestled in the Armed Forces Championships again. I was significantly better, but I had to wrestle three studs and I lost all three matches in the Greco-Roman tournament. I was good enough that Rob kept me around and let me compete a short time later at the U.S. Open in Las Vegas.

Rob sat me down after the Armed Forces tournament.

"You're making good progress, Adam," Coach Hermann said. "You're the most improved guy on the team."

Those words really resonated with me. I had made noticeable gains and it gave me a boost to know that my coach had recognized that.

I started the U.S. Open by winning my first match against a guy named Chris Meyer. I beat the guy by a couple of points. Next up was Josh Hall, the guy who had beaten me the year before. I had improved, but he was still really good and he kicked my butt again.

I definitely showed improvement and I was starting to mature physically because I was working hard.

After the 2001 U.S. Open, I went back to my unit and I was promoted to third-class petty officer. Rob knew that if I was going to become an elite wrestler, I had to train full-time.

Rob helped me gain a transfer to San Diego, where I joined the South Pacific (SOPAC) wrestling club. SOPAC was a feeder program for the All-Navy team and provided an opportunity to train full-time.

Overcoming Obstacles to Excel

SOPAC had some very good wrestlers that really helped me progress, including Kurt Kyle. Kurt was a Naval Academy graduate. He basically ran the team and he was a great leader.

Kurt was smaller than me, but stronger than me. He wrestled with me and pushed me as much as I could. I would eventually become too much for him to handle, but he never stopped trying.

For the next two years, I trained there and with the All-Navy team four months a year in Pensacola, Florida. That was my job with the military. I trained two or three times a day and focused on the process of improving. I had a few other duties, but 95 percent of the time I trained for wrestling.

It was exactly what I had hoped to do when I joined the Coast Guard.

I was training full-time in wrestling, and I continued to gain my confidence. I also was sharpening my mind and learning how to push myself to new limits.

The next season in 2002, at the Armed Forces Championships, I lost a one-point match to Jason Loukides. Jason competed at the World Championships. That built my confidence to the point where I started thinking about the Olympics as a possibility for me.

Later that year, I went to the Sunkist Kids tournament in Arizona and I ended up placing fourth. It was my first international tournament. I lost to Chael Sonnen for third place. Chael went on to excel in the UFC and is now a broadcaster for the sport on ESPN. I always wanted my rematch with Chael, but it never happened.

It was exciting to know that I had placed in a big tournament and my confidence continued to grow.

The next year, I beat Loukides by one point at the Armed Forces tournament in 2003. I placed second.

That win landed me a spot in the national rankings at No. 10 in my weight class.

I was wrestling full-time while making a good living in the military. I was earning a full-time salary plus insurance and benefits.

It was nice to finally have a little money in my pocket after growing up poor.

During my fourth season with the Navy, I was in Florida training

BELIEVE AND ACHIEVE

with Coach Rob Hermann.

In January 2003, I wanted to have a serious conversation with Rob.

I could've left the military in July 2003, and I put in an application with the Los Angeles Police Department.

I had a couple of big decisions to make. One of my goals was to become a police officer.

I really respected Rob's opinion, and he had coached several Olympians.

Rob and I were driving to New Orleans to work with some kids in the Gator Wrestling Club.

I was making steady progress in 2003, but I still hadn't qualified for the U.S. World Team Trials. I was ranked No. 10 in the country, but I wasn't quite ready to make a serious run at a World or Olympic Team.

I turned to Rob with a question.

"I want you to be honest with me," I said. "You aren't going to hurt my feelings. Is it actually possible for me to make the Olympics?"

Rob's response blew me away.

"Absolutely, I think you can make an Olympic Team," Rob said. "It's going to take a lot of work, but I think you can get there."

That conversation was huge for me.

And let me know the Olympics were a realistic goal.

I wasn't thinking it was going to happen in 2004, but I set my sights on making the Olympic Team in 2008.

Rob Hermann had such a huge impact on my wrestling career and my life.

He's the guy who gave me a chance to wrestle in the military and paved the way for me to pursue my dreams.

My teammate, Neal Rodak, also was encouraging me to wrestle in college. Neal was the best wrestler on the Navy team at that time and he already had his college degree.

My cousin, John Bailey, was a member of the LAPD and he encouraged me to get my education.

"Dude, you can become a cop anytime," John told me. "If you get a college education, you will definitely get hired by the LAPD."

Overcoming Obstacles to Excel

I received some great advice and that really helped me make my decision to keep wrestling and get an education.

It changed my whole world.

Because of Rob Hermann, I received a scholarship offer in 2003 to wrestle at the U.S. Olympic Education Center at Northern Michigan University. Rob also helped me gain a sponsor as I joined the Gator Wrestling Club.

The USOEC offered aspiring young Olympic athletes an opportunity to train and compete while receiving a college education.

It was the ideal place for many of the country's top Greco-Roman wrestlers to learn and develop. Most were guys coming straight out of high school.

I was a few years older than the typical freshman when I started at Northern Michigan.

I would wrestle at the USOEC for Coach Ivan Ivanov, one of the best Greco-Roman coaches in the world.

I was thinking about getting out of the military and Rob Hermann suggested that I join the USOEC program. Rob connected me with Ivan and then I also was able to join the Gator Wrestling Club.

Rob, Ivan and Momir Petkovic were my three main coaches at the Senior level and all of them were great.

Ivan was from Bulgaria and was a successful Greco-Roman wrestler on the Senior level. He had placed fifth at the Olympic Games.

Ivan had an incredible passion for wrestling. He was an old-school coach who before practice lined us up by weight class according to our ranking.

Practices were always based on what we needed to work on and improve on.

Our practices were two hours long and they were grueling. He really pushed us and challenged us.

If I was turned by a gut-wrench in a tournament, he would have me stay after practice and work on it. He would keep me there for two hours after our second practice of the day to work on it.

He didn't care how long it took or what it took. He would work with us every step of the way until we got it right. That's just Ivan.

BELIEVE AND ACHIEVE

He commanded respect from every guy in the room. He could also be your friend off the mat – he's a very friendly, engaging and genuinely nice guy. But when practice started, he was the coach and he was in charge.

Ivan would also get down on the mat and wrestle with the guys. I remember when he would wrestle with my teammate, Harry Lester. Harry was a very talented and explosive middleweight wrestler from Akron, Ohio. He was one of the nation's best recruits coming out of high school.

When Harry first came to Northern Michigan, Ivan would wrestle Harry and beat him even though Ivan was a lot older. Eventually, Harry started beating Ivan but Harry still had to work to beat him. Harry went on to win two bronze medals at the World Championships and became an Olympian in 2012.

Ivan pushed us hard. There is something special about him. He is an amazing coach. He put a lot of young guys on World and Olympic teams. It was just incredible what he did.

One of Ivan's wrestlers, Andy Bisek, was horrible when he came to Northern Michigan. He couldn't beat anybody. Andy's story was similar to mine. But Andy kept working hard and kept improving. And then after a few years with Ivan, Andy won two World medals and made an Olympic Team in 2016.

Andy is one of the guys I admire for how hard he worked. He never complained and he became one of the best wrestlers in the World.

Before I arrived at Northern Michigan, the USOEC already had a very good wrestler at my weight class in R.C. Johnson. As soon as I arrived, we trained together, pushed each other and made each other better. We really battled in practice and in competitions.

R.C. was a personable, friendly and likeable guy. And he also was very intelligent. Even though we were wrestling against each other we still managed to hit it off right away and become great friends.

I continued to improve and I defeated Dan Hicks at the Dave Schultz International in Colorado Springs. That was a big win. Dan was a guy that I really looked up to as a Greco wrestler. He was a tough, hard-nosed guy who had beaten me on a number of occasions.

I qualified for the U.S. Olympic Trials in 2004 at the RCA Dome in Indianapolis. I lost to Garrett Lowney, a 2000 Olympic bronze medalist who went on to make his second Olympic Team in 2004. He beat me pretty handily at the Trials. I had been training with him and we had a few close matches in practice. I wanted to beat him and I felt like I could, but he caught me with an arm throw and turned me with a gut-wrench. I tried to come back, but he was such a solid wrestler. He was just a better wrestler than me at that time.

Lowney's coach, Dan Chandler, told Coach Hermann that I could surprise some people at the Olympic Trials.

I had to wrestle Dan Hicks again, this time in the third-place match at the Olympic Trials.

He beat me this time and then he sat down on the mat after his hand was raised. He took off his shoes and left them on the center of the mat to signify his retirement. He walked off the mat and waved to the crowd as they gave him a standing ovation.

I wasn't even mad about losing at that moment because I had so much respect for Dan. It was a pretty cool moment for him and for everybody there.

I sat in the stands and watched the finals of the 2004 Olympic Trials in the RCA Dome. It was the first time where I felt like I wanted to be in the finals and I wish I would've been out there competing. I had the mindset of being a guy that wanted to be out there.

That day, I started thinking about the 2008 Olympic Trials. Lowney and Hicks retired in 2004, and Justin Ruiz was going to be the No. 1 guy going into the next Olympic cycle. Lowney beat Ruiz in the finals of the 2004 Olympic Trials.

I knew I would have an excellent opportunity if I continued to progress over the next four years.

I received my first taste of international travel in June 2004 when I wrestled at the University World Championships in Lodz, Poland.

I moved up to heavyweight for that tournament. I was coming off the Olympic Trials and I didn't have to cut any weight for University Worlds.

It was a good experience for me. I lost both of my matches, to

BELIEVE AND ACHIEVE

wrestlers from Hungary and Poland, and finished in 10th place. Looking back, I wish I would have taken that event a little more seriously. I was a little worn down from a long season and I knew it was going to be tough wrestling the bigger guys at heavyweight.

I wasn't as strong mentally as I needed to be, but it was a good trip for me.

Later in the year, I had the opportunity to compete internationally again when I wrestled at the World Cup in September 2004 in Tblisi, Georgia. Tblisi was part of the former Soviet Union and in a country that excelled in wrestling.

The World Cup is a dual-meet format and an annual event where the top countries wrestle against each other. That was an amazing opportunity for someone trying to gain experience.

Wrestling top-level international competition was a good way to measure myself with the new four-year Olympic cycle beginning.

I had never wrestled Greco-Roman growing up or in high school. Greco was all upper-body wrestling. You couldn't attack a wrestler's legs. When I was younger, I was afraid to try Greco. I saw a guy who was launched to his back one time and I decided I wasn't going to sign up for Greco. I would only be wrestling freestyle. I never dreamed I would become a top-level Greco-Roman wrestler.

I didn't wrestle my first Greco match until 2000, so it was pretty cool to see how far I had progressed in a short time. The good news was I still had plenty of room for improvement.

The 2004 World Cup was an interesting experience. During one of our practices, a fight broke out. Two of our lightweight wrestlers, Joe Warren and Lindsey Durlacher, got into a huge fist-fight. They were punching each other and didn't seem terribly worried that they might injure one of their teammates or themselves. They were going after each other and they were two tough, tenacious competitors who didn't back down from anybody. Joe went on to win a World title in 2006 and Lindsey won a World bronze medal that same year. Joe and Lindsey were the two smallest guys on the team, but they were fearless and would challenge anybody.

Joe Warren became a mixed martial arts champion for Bellator. He is a great fighter. He always possessed the mindset to fight.

Overcoming Obstacles to Excel

The World Cup was my first Senior-level tournament overseas. They had a huge crowd and the fans were into it. They were loud and very intense. It was a totally different culture than what we were used to.

I wrestled the Georgian, who was an Olympic silver medalist, and their fans were going crazy cheering for him. He reverse-lifted me into the air and then gently put me down on the mat onto my back. He scored a touch-fall over me. The guy was a monster and made me look like a little baby because he handled me so easily.

I remember they selected me for drug testing for some reason after the match and they didn't pick the Georgian. I didn't exactly look like the guy who was doing anything illegal while having my butt kicked in that match. There definitely was some corruption in the sport at times.

I ended up winning one match at the 2004 World Cup. I defeated a wrestler from France. We finished third as a team and Brad Vering went undefeated in that event. The U.S. team was very strong at that time.

Brad Vering was one of the best teammates I ever had. He was an awesome guy with a magnetic personality. I really looked up to him. He had a tremendous work ethic, one of the best on the team, and he was always doing extra workouts. And he was an intense competitor who was a heck of a wrestler. I learned a great deal from being around Brad and he had a huge impact on me after I moved to the Olympic Training Center.

The World Cup was an excellent measuring stick for me. I knew I was not even close to the top guys, but I was still confident that I would be that caliber of a wrestler at some point. I had already made huge improvements with my wrestling and I knew I still had plenty of room to become better.

The first time I wrestled Justin Ruiz, he beat me decisively by technical fall in the first period at the 2002 U.S. Open. I didn't know much about him at that time, but I was about to find out. After I wrestled him, I knew he was very good. He was super strong and very smart. And he was a very good technical wrestler.

In 2005, I was second at the World Team Trials behind Justin Ruiz. Justin went on to win a bronze medal that year at the World

BELIEVE AND ACHIEVE

Championships.

I was excited to return to the mat for the 2005-06 season after ascending to No. 2 on the U.S. ladder in Greco-Roman wrestling at 96 kilograms/211.5 pounds.

I was now a member of the U.S. National Team and I was receiving a monthly stipend of $1,000 from USA Wrestling for being No. 2 at my weight class.

I followed by placing fourth at the Trials in 2006. About a week before the Trials that year, I came down with food poisoning and that negatively affected my performance.

I lost to R.C. Johnson and Phil Johnston at the World Team Trials in 2006. Even though I was less than 100 percent physically in that tournament, it was still frustrating. I placed fourth at the Trials after finishing second the year before. It felt like a step back to me and I was eager to bounce back.

R.C. Johnson graduated from Northern Michigan in 2005 and moved to the Olympic Training Center in Colorado Springs. Most of the top Senior-level athletes in Greco-Roman trained at the OTC. Those wrestlers included resident-athletes at the Olympic Training Center along with a number of top wrestlers from the U.S. Army's World Class Athlete Program.

WCAP provided an excellent opportunity for athletes to receive funding to live and train as an Olympic-level wrestler. A number of elite WCAP wrestlers won medals at the Olympic and World level.

A year later, I followed R.C. Johnson to the Springs after I completed my degree in 2006.

R.C. was my favorite person to wrestle and my toughest opponent besides Justin Ruiz. R.C. and I had agreed that if either one of us made the Olympic Team we would take the other as a training partner. We became really good friends. And we made good on that Olympic promise as you will discover.

I graduated from Northern Michigan University with a bachelor's degree in criminal justice. I earned my degree in three years. I took extra classes in the evenings and online to achieve that.

Northern Michigan University was an interesting place to go to school and train. It is located in the Upper Peninsula on the shores of

Lake Superior. The school is in Marquette, a town of 21,000 people. For a kid who grew up in California, and then was stationed in Hawaii and San Diego, arriving at Northern Michigan was a huge culture shock for me.

The average temperature in the winter was in the 20s. Needless to say, we weren't playing any baseball in the winter in Michigan like we did in California. It also snowed often in Marquette and that was something new and foreign to me.

It was a huge adjustment for a California kid who grew up near an ocean. Now I was in the upper Midwest near a frozen lake by the Canadian border.

I hated the weather in Marquette, Michigan, but the experience there wasn't all bad.

I did not own a winter coat until I moved to Michigan. I ordered a coat online. I had never been in a cold place until I arrived there.

I didn't like the cold, but the worst part about Marquette was that it was dark, gray and cloudy all of the time. I was used to seeing the sun shine when I lived in California and in Hawaii.

I just wasn't a big fan of the weather there. I never got used to it during the three years I lived and trained there.

During my time at Northern Michigan, I did meet the love of my life.

Before I went to school at Northern Michigan, I had gone there to train and Ivan Ivanov introduced me to a girl in the cafeteria.

When I started school there in the fall of 2003, I saw the same girl again.

She was a member of the Northern Michigan soccer team. One day, their team was outside practicing when the wrestling team was also outside for a workout.

We would cross-train for wrestling practice by playing soccer and I went over to borrow a ball from the women's practice. The girl saw me and immediately pointed it out to one of her friends.

"That boy from the cafeteria is back!"

A short time later, she sent me an AOL instant message online while I was taking a test.

"Hey, how are you? This is Marley."

I responded right away.

"Hey, I'm Adam. I'm sorry I'm right in the middle of an online test. I will message you back when I'm done."

"Ok," she responded.

When I completed my online test, I quickly went to reply to her last AOL message.

But there was one problem. I accidentally deleted her message. This wasn't a good thing. At all.

It ended up taking me a couple of days to track down her screen name. I think she thought I was putting her off at first because I hadn't responded after my test.

I finally figured out her screen name and then messaged her back.

Shortly after that, I started dating Marley Garceo.

On our first few dates, I ended up hanging out with Marley and we invited her twin sister, Emily, to join us.

After a few dates, I asked Marley if it would be all right if just the two of us could go on a date. We really hit it off and had an instant connection.

In my opinion, she's a beautiful woman and I was very attracted to her. She seemed mature for her age. She was 20 years old when I met her. I was a little bit older because I had been in the military. I'm 2½ years older than Marley.

I had life experiences and I was making some money when I was in the Coast Guard. I was a little more mature than a lot of the other people I went to college with.

Marley was very focused on what she wanted to do. She wanted to be a teacher. We just really connected and I fell in love with her.

I wanted to spend all of the time I could with her. She was supportive of what I was doing. She was like-minded, as far as athletics. I watched her practice and she was one of the hardest workers on the team. And she played really hard and was one of the better soccer players on her team.

She totally understood the type of commitment it takes to be a successful athlete. We had that same mindset.

We just really clicked in every way. After our practices, we would go to the library together and study.

We never argued when we first started dating. In college, we only had one disagreement, but we were able to figure it out in a mature way and get past it.

After meeting Marley, Northern Michigan wasn't so bad after all. Marley was the best thing about the school. My wrestling experience there was great, and Ivan was amazing, but meeting Marley obviously topped all of that.

During our time in college, Marley and I went on a trip to Hawaii in 2004. We spent a week there. We went back to Hilo to see one of my buddies, Paul Caldentey, that I was in the Coast Guard with. To this day, Paul and I are still really good friends. I was a groomsman in his wedding.

Paul was a great host. We did a lot of great stuff during that trip. We had so much fun.

We hiked up to the top of Mount Mauna Kea. We visited the volcanoes. We hiked at Rainbow Falls, a spectacular place with some incredible waterfalls. We went camping on the beach. It was an amazing week for us. We went to the other side of the island to Kona, which is a little more popular side of the island.

That's what I love about Hawaii. There are so many wonderful activities to do. When I lived there, we were outside as much as we could to enjoy the beautiful weather and the scenery. I tried to maximize the time I was there. And experience everything I could see and do.

During the summer of 2005, one of the biggest events in my life occurred.

Marley was home for the summer with her family in Denver and I devised a secret plan with the help of my good friend, Neal Rodak.

I told Neal what I was planning on doing and he was totally on board with helping me. I was still living and training in Michigan, but I was going to come back to Colorado to propose to Marley.

Neal agreed to let me stay at his house in Colorado Springs during my trip there.

I started putting my master plan into action when I called Marley.

"Let's go on a date. And by the way, you have to wear a nice dress."

I went out and bought a nice suit to wear on the date. I didn't have any idea how to tie a tie, but fortunately my teammate Russ Davie did and taught me how.

Marley knew right away, or at least she thought she knew, that I was going to propose to her.

I took her to the Penrose Room, a five-star restaurant at the beautiful Broadmoor Hotel and Resort in Colorado Springs. We enjoyed an amazing dinner that night.

In my eyes, everything went according to plan.

But it didn't go quite the way Marley had expected it to.

I didn't propose that night.

She wouldn't say it, but I could sense that she was a little bummed. She wears her emotions on her sleeve and I could see she was disappointed.

My goal wasn't to upset her or make her feel badly.

But at the same time, my plan was working perfectly.

I knew what I was going to do next.

We woke up early the next day and we planned to hike to the top of Pikes Peak.

I asked Marley's family and one of my best friends, Aaron Wintterle, to drive to the top of Pikes Peak and wait for us.

We left bright and early. Along the hike, I was dropping a few hints to Marley.

"Do you think a hike is like a good relationship, where it has ups and downs, but in the end, you finish together?" I told her.

She didn't say anything, but I could tell from the look on her face that she was probably thinking, "What the hell is he talking about?"

About nine miles up the mountain, I had found the ideal spot.

The time was right for me to make my move.

I dropped down on one knee.

I was nervous and my heart was pounding.

I thought about a more elaborate proposal, but I ended up keeping it simple and getting right to the point.

I pulled a sparkling diamond ring out of my backpack and I showed it to her.

"Will you marry me?" I said, looking up and into her eyes.

"Yes!" Marley responded immediately.

Smiles spread across our faces and we embraced before Marley became emotional and started crying.

The Pikes Peak Marathon was going on that day and one of the runners was passing by. He saw Marley become emotional right after I proposed.

The runner thought something might be wrong.

He stopped and asked her, "Are you all right?"

"We're getting married!" she said enthusiastically.

"Congratulations!" the man responded before turning back to resume his race.

That made us all laugh during one of the happiest moments of my life.

The whole time we were climbing Pikes Peak I knew Marley's family and my buddy were waiting for us at the top with champagne to celebrate with us.

Marley was a cardio machine. Not only was she a college soccer player, she had done several half marathons.

It's a 13-mile hike to the top of Pikes Peak, and somewhere around mile 11, I was starting to struggle. I was having headaches as we continued to climb to a higher elevation. I was living in Michigan at the time, so I wasn't used to the Colorado climate.

We were in thin air and the altitude was having a negative effect on me.

Pikes Peak is 14,114-feet high and we had been training at sea level in Michigan. The elevation in Marquette was around 650 feet.

As we neared the finish of our hike, it looked like a storm was rolling in and I was still having some difficulty.

Marley was encouraging me, "C'mon, we need to finish this!"

Her family was making bets during our hike that Marley wasn't going to be able to finish, but I was actually having more trouble than her.

I was a World-class athlete, but she was kicking my butt a little bit that day.

As we neared the top of Pikes Peak, Marley spotted my buddy.

BELIEVE AND ACHIEVE

"Hey, that's Aaron!" she said.

Then she saw her family and everyone let out a cheer as we approached.

We popped a bottle of champagne and everybody was hugging each other.

It was an amazing moment even though I was drained from the hike.

It was an awesome day and my proposal plan had worked to near-perfection.

And luckily for me, I started feeling better on the way back down the mountain.

It was a memorable day.

And she said, "Yes!"

I was going to marry the love of my life.

Less than a year later, in 2006, Marley and I graduated from college and then we moved together to Colorado Springs.

We went from dark, dreary days in Michigan to the sunshine and spectacular scenery in one of the country's most breathtaking cities.

Colorado Springs is a popular tourist destination that has grown to half a million people. The Rocky Mountains run parallel and just to the west of the city, with snow-capped Pikes Peak standing out in a majestic setting.

It's not as warm as California, but the winters in the Springs are much milder than in Michigan. The sun is shining virtually every day. The Springs is an outdoor paradise with plenty of places to hike, camp and fish.

Colorado Springs is less than an hour drive from Marley's hometown of Denver, a metropolitan area of more than a million people.

When Marley and I moved to Colorado Springs, we rented a townhouse from my friend Neal Rodak, who was dating Marley's twin sister, Emily. Neal and Emily eventually married. They now have four children and live in California. Rob Hermann tries to take credit for their marriage, but secretly I know it was me.

I married Marley on July 6, 2007, in Golden, Colorado, located just outside Denver. We found a beautiful place in Golden where we were married outdoors. It was a very cool setting for our wedding ceremony.

Overcoming Obstacles to Excel

My younger brother, William, was my best man and my sister, Leslie, was a bridesmaid.

It was awesome having them share this special day with me.

We faced our share of adversity growing up and the three of us developed a close bond during those challenging times.

My brother has a black belt in Jiu Jitsu and he was a mixed martial arts fighter. William actually introduced me to Jiu Jitsu.

My brother was diagnosed with lung cancer in 2014. He had two-thirds of his lung removed. He is now cancer-free and is competing again. He has a good, stable job and is doing well.

William is 14 months younger than me and he grew up facing many of the same hardships that I did.

Leslie is the youngest and she had to put up with two older brothers. She's also doing well with her life and her career.

I'm very proud of them.

I have good relationships with my siblings.

We had a rough upbringing, but we fought through it.

CHAPTER 3
Breakthrough in Baku

I came back strong during the 2007 season. I continued to improve and I finished second at the U.S. Open to 2005 World bronze medalist Justin Ruiz.

Justin swept me by identical 3-0, 3-0 scores in the finals at the Las Vegas Convention Center.

He was able to turn me and I was unable to turn him in the par terre position down on the mat.

That was the difference in the match.

At that time, each wrestler would have an opportunity in the top position to turn his opponent. If the top wrestler was unable to execute a turn, the bottom man would be awarded a point.

I had lost to Justin again, but I had beaten him a couple of times before that in regular-season tournaments. I knew I was capable of defeating him when it counted most. I just hadn't done it yet.

Justin had won a majority of our matches and he had always defeated me when the stakes were highest. In 2007, he was more consistent and had a more solid foundation than I did.

I was well aware that I still had work to do. But I felt like I was closing the gap and that I could eventually beat him. He was a very good wrestler. He was one of the best guys in the World. He had won a medal at the World Championships for a reason. He was really good. And he had been very successful against international competition.

I received another shot at Justin when I advanced to face him in the finals of the 2007 U.S. World Team Trials in Las Vegas.

BELIEVE AND ACHIEVE

Justin had been a fixture as the No. 1 guy in the U.S. in Greco-Roman wrestling at 211.5 pounds and it was going to take a strong effort to knock him off.

The entire American Greco squad was very good. The U.S. team was coming off a respectable third-place finish at the 2006 World Championships in China. The American team actually was in position to win the team title that year before just coming up short. That was a great sign as we continued to move closer to the 2008 Olympic year.

Joe Warren had won a World title for the U.S. in 2006 with Lindsey Durlacher and Harry Lester capturing bronze medals for the American team.

I entered the finals of the 2007 U.S. World Team Trials with the mindset that I could finally break through and beat Justin Ruiz.

I would face him in a best-of-3 match series with the winner earning a berth to the World Championships.

In those days, matches also used a best-of-3 period format. A wrestler needed to win two of the three periods to prevail.

In 2007, both of the matches I had with Justin would go the full three periods.

In the first match, Justin came out strong and won the first period 3-0. I won the second period 1-1 on criteria. Neither of us were able to secure a turn and I won by virtue of scoring last. The same thing happened in the third period when neither of us could score a turn. Justin scored last in a 1-1 bout, so he won the final period on criteria to win the first match.

He won a coin flip in the third period that allowed him to be in the down position last.

A lot of people didn't like the rules they had back then. I liked wrestling down on the mat in par terre and I was always confident when competing with those rules.

I wasn't crazy that matches would sometimes come down to a ball draw or a coin flip.

It does seem silly that Olympic bouts and matches of this magnitude would come down to flipping a coin or pulling a ball out of a bag. But that was the reality during that Olympic cycle.

FILA, wrestling's international governing body, was known for its unconventional methods. FILA's rationale and way of operating weren't overly popular at times with USA Wrestling, the national governing body for wrestling in this country.

A lot of what FILA was doing came under plenty of scrutiny because it didn't make a whole lot of sense. And there were plenty of rumors about possible corruption going on within that organization.

Unfortunately, with those rules, the best wrestler didn't always win in Greco-Roman wrestling. If a wrestler had good defense and could avoid being turned, he would gamble that the coin flip or the ball draw would go his way. If it did, he had to avoid being scored upon in the last 30 seconds to prevail.

That happened frequently in those days.

Down one match to none in the finals of the 2007 World Team Trials, I knew I had to come out strong in the second match against Justin Ruiz. I couldn't let the matches come down to coin flips or criteria. I had to make something happen.

I took charge early in the second match and scored a 6-0 win in the first period. I scored a takedown and I was able to turn him a couple of times. I dominated that period.

Now I needed to win one of the final two periods to win the second match and extend the series to a third and deciding bout.

But Justin, being the great competitor that he is, found a way to come back on me. He won the final two periods 3-0, 3-0 to win the second match.

I set a really fast pace in the first period of our second match, but I couldn't maintain it in the last two periods as fatigue set in. I knew I needed to do extra workouts so that wouldn't happen again.

Justin Ruiz had landed a spot on the 2007 U.S. World Team. He made another United States World Team. And I had finished second once again.

It was disappointing. I was upset. I walked back to the warmup area shaking my head in disbelief. I was frustrated and angry. I wanted to make that team, but I also knew my Olympic dream was very much alive.

I never accepted losing, I was never OK with it. I felt like I was training harder and eating better than everyone and wondered why I wasn't winning.

I talked to my wife about it.

"Why am I losing?" I said to my wife. "I feel like I am working hard enough to win."

"Why don't you just pick him up and throw him," Marley said, "then pick him up and throw him again?"

That made me laugh and put a smile on my face. I wish it was that easy to do.

I appreciated her being supportive and calming me down.

There were so many times when I was frustrated or down when Marley would say something to make me feel better. She was the perfect partner for me on my Olympic journey.

I wasn't initially picked to be a training partner for the 2007 U.S. World Team in Greco-Roman even though I was the No. 2 guy in my weight class. The No. 1 guy wasn't required to take the No. 2 wrestler as a training partner. And that made sense because those wrestlers may have been heated rivals who have no desire to train with each other.

Justin Ruiz didn't pick me to go to the Worlds in 2007 and I don't blame him. If it was me, I probably wouldn't have picked Justin either because he was my main competition.

The seven Greco-Roman athletes who made the World Team were allowed to choose their own training partners for the trip to the 2007 World Championships in Baku, Azerbaijan.

A training partner plays an important role, serving not only as a practice partner for the World Team member but also providing support for that wrestler. A good training partner offers words of encouragement and is there to help the No. 1 guy with whatever he needs to prepare for competition. That may be anything from sitting in the sauna to assisting the World Team member as he cuts weight. Or it may be hanging out with the top guy to keep him company while passing the time between workouts.

The experience is beneficial for the training partner because he has the opportunity to witness the experience and see what it is like at a big event like the World Championships or the Olympics.

He also receives a chance to continue training against top-flight wrestlers.

Overcoming Obstacles to Excel

Training partners are often young wrestlers on the verge of making a World or Olympic team. A number of training partners from the 2007 World Team went on to make World and Olympic teams for the U.S. in the years that followed.

Being around the World Championships can provide huge inspiration and motivation for a training partner when they resume their own training for the following season.

And that's why I wanted to make the trip to Baku for the World Championships. I talked to Jim Ravannack, the head of the Gator Wrestling Club. I wrestled for the Gator club and Jim was gracious enough to agree to pay my way to go to Azerbaijan so I could serve as a training partner for the American team.

It would turn out to be a worthwhile investment. It was an amazing opportunity that would eventually pay significant dividends for me.

And pave the way for me to achieve my goals. I was well aware that going to the World Championships and witnessing the competition there in person would allow me to see what I needed to do and where I needed to go to reach that level.

Baku was not an easy place to travel to. It is halfway around the globe from the United States. Most people in the U.S. probably have never heard of Azerbaijan and have no idea where it is located.

Of course, there are no direct flights from Colorado Springs to Baku. I had to drive a little over an hour to Denver, fly 10 hours to Frankfurt, Germany and then fly another four hours to Baku, Azerbaijan.

It was a long trip, but it was definitely worth it. International travel is a way of life for Senior-level wrestlers. It can be grueling and exhausting at times, but luckily for us we were able to find plenty to do on an overseas trip.

We would watch movies and television shows on the plane. We listened to music. We read books and magazines. And we would walk around and talk to the other athletes on the flight.

We would also be served one, and often times two, hot meals on the flight. That definitely helped.

And we would sleep. Those trips were tough on the sleep schedule, so we would try to rest as much as we could on those marathon flights.

Our teams typically arrived more than a week before competition to acclimate and adjust to the time change.

The time in Baku is 11 hours ahead of the time in Colorado, so it took a few days for our bodies to adapt to the new time zone.

The quality of the food often is another issue you encounter when going to a foreign country. Other countries often use different seasonings and spices in their food than we do back home, and some of their cuisine doesn't always agree with us.

The food in Baku wasn't the best, but it was just another obstacle that we faced. If you like rice, Baku is the place for you because they eat a lot of it there.

Training and competing away from home can present its share of challenges.

Azerbaijan is an eastern European country that is part of the former Soviet Union. It is an old Russian republic in an ancient city. Wrestling is a huge deal in Azerbaijan and the country has fared well in wrestling at top international competitions in the styles of Greco-Roman and freestyle.

Baku is a bustling city of just over two million people and is situated on the shores of the Caspian Sea. The place we stayed, an old Russian hotel known as the Hotel Absheron, was located about two blocks away from the Caspian Sea.

Our hotel was the main headquarters for the World Championships. Wrestlers from other countries were staying there as well. Media from the U.S. and other nations also were in our hotel.

Safety is always an issue when you are competing internationally and the folks in Baku did what they could to protect us. We had four uniformed military personnel, armed with machine guns, stationed outside our hotel during our time there. They were young soldiers from the Azerbaijan Army.

We knew first-hand how scary it can be to travel overseas.

I was at the Pan American Championships in Rio de Janeiro, Brazil in 2006 when something unfortunate happened to one of our coaches.

Overcoming Obstacles to Excel

Our coach was out having a drink and he was talking with some of the Brazilians. He was wearing an expensive Rolex watch and someone put something in his drink.

He was drugged and then mugged. He woke up in the street and he had been beat up. His Rolex was gone and so was all of his money. He nearly died. He was taken to the emergency room at a local hospital before he was eventually allowed to fly back to the U.S.

The U.S. Olympic Committee and USA Wrestling would talk to the athletes about being careful when going to a foreign country. Being safe and using common sense is paramount.

It can be dangerous and scary at times when you travel internationally. You don't want to go anywhere alone.

The old hotel we stayed at in Baku certainly had its share of challenges. Hot water was at a premium. If your roommate showered before you, chances were good that your shower may not be hot or even warm. An ice-cold shower is not a fun way to start the day.

The water quality often isn't the best outside the U.S., so we would use bottled water to brush our teeth.

In one of the rooms, a wrestler tapped the wall with his foot and dust came flying down the side of the wall.

Living conditions aren't always ideal when you travel halfway around the world for a wrestling tournament.

You can't let distractions like that disrupt your focus. Adversity is a way of life at times when you venture overseas. You have to expect challenges when you don't have all of the comforts of home.

While in Baku, the city was having its share of issues. Baku is a large industrial city that is ranked as one of the most-polluted cities in the world. The air quality was not the best.

Fortunately, we didn't spend a lot of time outside. We were training and competing indoors during our trip to Baku.

I was there as a training partner, but I was also there to improve as a wrestler as I continued my quest to make the 2008 Olympic Team.

On the trip, I wrestled a lot with World champion Dremiel Byers, the heavyweight on the U.S. team. Dremiel brought his Army teammate, Phil Johnston, as his training partner, so I was able to train with Phil almost every day.

BELIEVE AND ACHIEVE

Byers was a big, strong, physical wrestler who was a tough, hard-nosed competitor. He also was an explosive athlete who moved very well for his size.

Dremiel was a tough matchup and it showed. He went on to win gold, silver and bronze medals at the World Championships. He also made two Olympic teams.

Wrestling with Dremiel was a great experience for me. I obviously wouldn't face anybody that big or strong in my weight class.

I also sat in the sauna to help American Brad Vering cut weight and get ready for his competition. I tried to provide encouragement for the guys competing and at the same time I was taking in the entire experience. I tried to study every aspect of what athletes were doing to prepare for this event.

I knew after spending time with Brad that he was ready. Brad was a professional, a veteran who had already been an Olympian in 2004. He had made numerous World teams and you could see how focused he was. He was primed to have a great performance as he pursued his first World medal.

When competition approached, we ventured to the venue for weigh-ins. Athletes made weight in the afternoon and then started competition the following morning.

I recognized a number of guys in line for the weigh ins at my weight class of 96 kilograms. I had beaten a number of them in competition. That was a good feeling. That gave me a boost, knowing that I had defeated some of the guys competing at the World Championships.

I knew I was good enough to be standing in that line for weigh-ins.

When the wrestling competition started, I sat in the stands at the spacious Ali Aliyev Arena and my foremost objective was to watch as many of the matches as I could at my weight class. I studied wrestlers, watching their styles and their tendencies.

I also watched the wrestlers in other weight classes.

The competition was excellent and the American team was off to a strong start in Greco.

They had great crowds in Baku, totaling around 10,000 fans for some sessions, at the 2007 World Championships. They were loud and enthusiastic.

They went crazy when a wrestler from Azerbaijan would take the mat. They would boo just as loud when a wrestler from neighboring Armenia would compete.

The two nations hated each other. They had been at war with each other on numerous occasions and that strained their diplomatic relations.

The loudest cheers of the week came when an Armenian lost and the large contingent of Azerbaijan fans stood and cheered.

The trip to Baku was my first time going to a World Championships. I watched everyone in my weight class. I watched as much wrestling as I could. It was awesome. It was an incredible atmosphere.

I was there and I was part of the U.S. Team, but at the same time I wasn't a part of it.

I was a spectator when our team wrestled. And that motivated me because I wanted to be out there wrestling.

At the same time, it was exciting to see our team doing well.

Brad Vering went on a huge roll and made it to the finals before winning a silver medal. It was Brad's first World medal. He was deserving because I knew how hard he worked and how dedicated he was. Everything was clicking for Brad that day.

He lost to a very tough Russian named Aleksey Mishin in the finals at 84 kilograms. Mishin had won an Olympic gold medal in 2004.

Brad gave a great effort before coming up just short in the gold-medal match. He had an amazing tournament and landed a well-deserved spot on the medal podium.

Lindsey Durlacher finished in fifth place and Harry Lester followed by winning a bronze medal for the U.S.

Those finishes were important because the top six wrestlers in each weight class qualified their country for the 2008 Olympic Games in those divisions.

One of the divisions we didn't qualify in was my weight class of 96 kilograms. Justin Ruiz won his first match at the Worlds, but lost his next two. He finished 13th.

Fortunately for us, there were other qualifiers for the Olympics so we still had opportunities to qualify my weight class.

It was an exciting few days as we were locked in a tight battle with Russia in the team race.

Dremiel Byers delivered a clutch performance to win his bronze-medal match. That gave us a one-point lead in the team race. The U.S. was looking to win a World team title in Greco-Roman wrestling for the first time.

We had a chance to make history.

Our fate would come down to the heavyweight bout between Cuba's Mijain Lopez and Russia's Khassan Baroev.

We needed Lopez, who would go on to win five World titles and three Olympic gold medals, to beat the Russian to give us the team title.

I wrestled the 6-foot-6, 300-pound Lopez in practice and it was obvious why he was so good. I felt completely overmatched. He was so big and strong, and he had 50 pounds on me. Lopez also was very athletic and could move extremely well for his size. He was on a whole different level. He was so elusive for a big guy. He had really good movement.

Vering told me that when they were training in Cuba, Lopez climbed a rope all the way to the top of a large gymnasium with a high ceiling and his legs never touched the rope. That's an incredible feat for a man that size.

Lopez was the only guy I had ever seen that made our heavy-weight, Dremiel Byers, look small. Byers was a big dude, but Lopez was huge. He looked like he could've played in the National Football League with his size, strength and athleticism.

I think Lopez is the best heavyweight wrestler ever. Alexander Karelin of Russia won three Olympic gold medals at heavyweight and he was a very strong wrestler. But Lopez was the best all-around wrestler. He was in a league of his own.

As great as Lopez was, there were still concern about him from the U.S. camp entering his finals match at the 2007 World Championships.

Overcoming Obstacles to Excel

There were rumors that Lopez had taken a payoff and thrown his finals match to Russia the year before at the 2006 World Championships in Guangzhou, China.

He had been turned numerous times, something that didn't seem possible, in that "loss" to the Russian in 2006. Lopez was too good to have been legitimately turned like that.

The entire Cuban team walked out of the venue after Lopez lost in 2006. They weren't too pleased with the way that match unfolded.

It's disgusting to see a guy who is working and training so hard throw a match like that. It's difficult to believe someone would do that, but it's a reality.

We were hoping history wasn't about to repeat itself.

The 2007 heavyweight finals match started at heavyweight and Lopez took control. You could sense right away after the first whistle that he was going to win the match.

Time was running out and our small American contingent started our own countdown:

"Five, four, three, two, one…"

The horn sounded.

And the match ended.

Lopez had finished off the win and we were all going crazy, jumping up and down while high-fiving and hugging.

We had edged Russia by one point to win the World team title.

That was an incredible moment for the U.S. Greco-Roman program. It was exciting and it was huge for our country. We were the best team in the world.

We won the World Championships as a team.

For the first time in U.S. history.

It was awesome. I was so happy for all of those guys and I was happy for the guy at my weight class, Justin Ruiz.

It also was monumental for Greco-Roman wrestling in the U.S. We would often take a backseat to freestyle in our own country, but not on this day. Greco was king on this magical day in Baku.

Just seconds after the final match ended, I remember our smallest guy, Lindsey Durlacher, running up and jumping into the arms of the massive Lopez.

BELIEVE AND ACHIEVE

The 300-pound Lopez had a huge smile on his face as he carried the 125-pound Durlacher around like he was a little kid.

Lopez was a guy our team knew well. He had trained in the U.S. and we saw him at a lot of the same tournaments. It was great to see how happy he was and it was great to see him come through to help us win the team title.

A few hours later, my mind was racing. I started thinking that as a competitor, and someone who was so close to making the team, I wanted to be out there wrestling for my country.

It was an amazing moment when the U.S. won the World team title. The team posed for numerous photographs with the championship trophy. I was in one photo that included wrestlers, coaches, training partners and everyone else from the U.S. traveling party. It was a very cool moment.

It was huge to be part of a historic moment and hear the Star-Spangled Banner being played after Coach Steve Fraser was awarded the championship trophy.

They were having trouble playing our national anthem in the arena, so Dremiel Byers started singing it and the rest of the U.S. team joined in.

A short time later, the song came on in the arena and our national anthem went out on the loudspeakers.

After the tournament, we went out to a nice restaurant and our awesome team leader, John Bardis, treated us to a victory dinner. We ate, drank and celebrated the landmark victory for the U.S.

We came back to the hotel and gathered in the lobby for more celebrating. We sat on large couches and chairs around a huge table in the middle of the lobby. The team trophy was placed on the center of the table for everyone that walked by to see.

John ordered a round of beer, and then another. And then another. We sat around for hours – talking, laughing, drinking, telling stories and enjoying ourselves.

It was a great chance for us to unwind after a memorable couple of days.

I remember a few of the rare times when it was actually fairly quiet during our late-night party.

That's when Fraser would raise both arms and call out, "World Champs!"

Our group erupted in cheers and it put a smile on our faces.

Hearing Fraser say that never got old.

Fraser won an Olympic gold medal for the U.S. in Greco-Roman wrestling in 1984. He also was in the corner coaching Rulon Gardner when he scored a stunning upset over three-time Olympic gold medalist Alexander Karelin of Russia in the 2000 Olympic finals.

Rulon's victory was one of the biggest upsets in Olympic history in any sport. He was a huge underdog and pulled off a tremendous upset to beat a legend in Karelin.

Seven years later, Fraser helped the U.S. Greco program achieve the unthinkable again.

We earned another victory that many people didn't think was possible.

It was a historic night in Baku.

Fraser brought a lot of intangibles that I liked in a coach.

He had the mindset of being tough and being the king of the wrestling room. He liked developing that hard-nosed wrestler. Those intense workouts that Fraser loved were beneficial for me during my time at the Olympic Training Center.

He loved grind matches in which we would wrestle live for long periods. He believed that would build your mental toughness and it did for me.

He made sure we were going to be in peak physical condition.

Coach Fraser wanted us to compete as much as we could and get as many matches in as possible, especially overseas where many of the top European countries excelled in Greco.

He wanted us to gain that level of experience. He was a big contributor in helping build my mental strength.

Fraser cared very deeply about the Greco-Roman wrestling program and the 2007 World team title meant a lot to him. He had put a number of years into making that goal become a reality.

By the time the party at the hotel started to wind down, it was the wee hours of the morning and the sun was starting to rise in Baku. And there were still about 20 full glasses of beer sitting on that large table

BELIEVE AND ACHIEVE

in the lobby.

You don't win a team title at the World Championships every day, especially for a U.S. team in Greco-Roman, and we got our money's worth with our celebration that night.

It was a fun night, one I will never forget. And it was a night that inspired me and lit a fire under me going into 2008.

It was hugely important for me to go to the World Championships in 2007. I was a training partner and I didn't compete, but the entire experience was incredibly valuable and beneficial.

I already was motivated, but going to that event brought my motivation up another level. I knew what I was capable of. I saw World medalists I had beaten that were competing for other countries.

I already knew I belonged in a tournament like that, but being there in person confirmed it for me.

When I arrived back home in the United States, I was ready to get back on the mat immediately and start training. And I did. I was serious about my goals and I wanted to maximize the time I had.

My focus had shifted to making the 2008 United States Olympic Team in Greco-Roman wrestling.

I knew it was a realistic goal for me now.

And I was going to do everything in my power to make that happen.

CHAPTER 4
Trials and Jubilation

I went right back to work after we made the long journey home from the 2007 World Championships in Baku, Azerbaijan. Watching that event raised my level of motivation to make the 2008 United States Olympic Team in Greco-Roman wrestling.

A month after the Worlds, I returned to competition at the 2007 Sunkist Kids International in Tempe, Arizona.

The Sunkist tournament was the kickoff event to the 2007-08 season for U.S. Senior-level wrestlers.

I advanced to the finals and edged R.C. Johnson to capture the title at 96 kilograms.

It was another low-scoring match that ended with scores of 1-1, 1-1. I won the bout on criteria.

I had to battle R.C. again a month later at the New York AC International in New York City.

We met in the semis and R.C. beat me 4-0, 1-1. I came back to down another familiar foe, Phil Johnston, in the third-place bout.

Justin Ruiz defeated R.C. 2-0, 2-0 in the finals.

It was good having a couple of tournaments to compete in after returning from Baku.

I was excited to get back on the mat. R.C. was one of my toughest rivals. It was hard for us to score points when we squared off. I knew what he liked to do and he knew what moves I excelled with.

R.C. was a good wrestler. He was one of the most talented guys we had. That was evident when he went on to make the U.S. World Team in 2009.

BELIEVE AND ACHIEVE

Phil Johnston was another one of my toughest opponents. The first time I wrestled him, he teched me and kicked my butt. Phil was a monster who Rob Hermann and I called "The Hulk." He had massive legs and was as strong as he looked.

It took me a year or two before I could finally beat him. Phil was always a good training partner for me.

We really pushed each other. He was a darn good wrestler in a deep weight class. Unfortunately for Phil, he was injured and was unable to compete at the 2008 Olympic Trials.

When the calendar flipped to 2008, the United States still hadn't qualified for the Olympic Games in my weight class of 96 kilograms/211.5 pounds.

And I was well aware of that.

Our best opportunity would come in February. The U.S. would be hosting the Pan American Championships at the Olympic Training Center in Colorado Springs.

The Pan American countries from North and South America would compete in a continental qualifier to determine an Olympic berth in each of the seven weight classes in Greco.

Justin Ruiz was No. 1 on the ladder and he would take the mat for the U.S. at the Pan American Championships.

Justin rolled to a pair of falls and a technical fall in his first three bouts. He advanced to face Cuba's Yosvani Goicochea in the match for the gold medal. Justin needed a victory to clinch our spot in the Olympics at 96 kilos.

Justin dropped the first period 2-1, but he stormed back to win the final two periods 3-2, 4-1. He had come through and delivered with a clutch performance.

He had qualified the United States for the Olympic Games at 211.5 pounds.

Fortunately for me and the other guys in the weight class, Justin still had to win the Olympic Trials to earn a trip to Beijing, China for the 2008 Olympic Games.

Before my weight class was qualified, I was starting to become a little bit nervous and anxious. I admit it was stressing me out to some extent. I was wondering if I might have to move up to heavyweight because we had already qualified for the Olympics in that division.

I knew Justin could beat the Cuban, but nothing is guaranteed. There was a lot of pressure on Justin to win those matches and it was nerve-wracking for me even though I wasn't wrestling.

If we didn't qualify for the Olympics at 96 kg, my chances of making the team at heavyweight weren't great. And there was no way I could cut down to 84 kg, another weight class the U.S. had already qualified for Beijing.

When Justin won the Pan Am Championships, I wasn't there. I was preparing to wrestle in the 2008 World Cup.

When I heard the news that Justin had qualified the weight class for Beijing, I was really happy. And relieved.

My chances of the Olympics were still alive. I knew I wasn't the favorite, but I still had an opportunity to achieve my Olympic dream.

My plan was to be done wrestling in 2008 whether I made the Olympic Team or not.

This was my last shot.

I had started 2008 by placing second at the Dave Schultz Memorial International in early February at the Olympic Training Center.

Justin Ruiz scored a 3-0, 1-1, 3-0 win over me in the finals.

He was able to turn me in the first and third periods. He had a good gut-wrench to one side that I was working on trying to stop.

My main focus became my gut-wrench defense in par terre. I had to stop him from turning me or I wasn't going to make the Olympic Team.

I received another opportunity to battle top international competition when I competed at the Greco-Roman World Cup in February 2008 in Szombathely, Hungary.

I went 2-1 during the event, earning wins over Hungary and South Korea. I lost a match to Iran.

I had a solid performance and that competition definitely gave me a boost.

I earned a huge win over Balasz Kiss in the dual meet against Hungary.

I hit a reverse lift and threw him, but they didn't give me the points. They blew the whistle for me to stop as he was flying through the air.

We were wrestling in his home country. You never know what is going to happen with the officiating sometimes.

I won that match against Kiss, so I wasn't too worried about being robbed of the points that I should have scored.

Kiss was short, stocky and powerful. He was an excellent wrestler whose long and storied career was still going when he competed at the World Championships in 2018. It's crazy to think that guys my age are still competing at the top level.

When the match against Kiss ended and my hand was raised, there wasn't a big celebration by me. I knew it was a pretty big win, but as I walked off the mat the heavyweights were walking out for the final match of the dual.

Looking back, it was a huge victory for me. Kiss went on to win the World Championships the next year in 2009. He beat Jimmy Lidberg of Sweden in the finals. I had earned a win over Lidberg a few years before.

Jimmy capped his career by winning an Olympic bronze medal in 2012. Not a bad way to finish a wrestling career, if you ask me.

The World Cup was a great experience for me and I was ready to resume my training back home.

My confidence just kept growing and I continued to build momentum as we moved closer to the U.S. Open and the Olympic Trials.

When I moved to the United States Olympic Training Center in Colorado Springs, Colorado in 2006, I connected with another coach who made a huge impact on my career.

That coach was Momir Petkovic, the long-time Assistant National Coach for the U.S. Greco-Roman Team.

Momir won a gold medal in Greco-Roman wrestling for the former Yugoslavia at the 1976 Olympic Games in Montreal.

Momir had come to the U.S. many years before he started coaching me. He had worked as a New York City taxi driver for a short time before he became a coach for Greco-Roman wrestlers in the United States.

Overcoming Obstacles to Excel

Momir was a unique and interesting character, to say the least. He grew up in Serbia and he possessed a thick eastern European accent. Even though he spoke pretty good English, it was hard to understand him at times. Over time, it did become easier.

Momir was a no-nonsense coach with a hard-nosed, intense approach. He was somebody who would tell it exactly like it was. He would never mince words. He also was a caring, compassionate coach who was completely invested in his athletes. He wanted the very best for them and was committed to making it happen.

If you worked hard and bought into what he was teaching, Momir would be your biggest ally and your biggest supporter.

And he had an Olympic gold medal. Momir had won at the highest level and he knew what it took to be the best. He was the No. 1 wrestler in the world in 1976 and he had the gold medal to prove it. That commanded an instant level of respect in my mind.

Momir and Ivan Ivanov were very similar in many ways.

I was very blessed to have three really good coaches – Momir, Ivan and Rob Hermann – who worked closely with me and were in my corner during my Greco-Roman career.

Momir loved making his points and then adding, "That's part of the deal."

He also would crack me up with the language he used. Momir used more than his share of profanity to make his point. Not in a demeaning way, it was just part of the way he spoke.

When he was upset with a call, he could light up a referee with the best of them while using his unique brand of English.

He also had the best moustache in wrestling. Momir had a bristly, thick, full old-school moustache that the Marlboro Man and actor Sam Elliott would have been proud of. That 'stache was his trademark.

Momir once shared a story that he had decided to shave off his moustache after having it for decades. Immediately after he shaved, he saw one of his grandkids. Momir said his new look scared his grandson and the young boy began to cry. Momir grew back his moustache.

Fortunately for me, Momir and I clicked right away after I

moved to the Olympic Training Center. He was the perfect guy to be in my corner after I had worked for another excellent coach, Ivan Ivanov, at the USOEC in Northern Michigan.

Momir was an amazing dude. There was never a dull moment when he was around. The guy was in his 50s and still in phenomenal shape. He would do workouts and climb the Manitou Incline with us.

Momir loved beating the wrestlers up the Incline and he did exactly that on numerous occasions.

The Incline was a walking trail that went straight up the Rocky Mountains and was located just outside Colorado Springs in the popular tourist destination of Manitou Springs. Over the course of climbing the Incline, the trail gains nearly 2,000 feet of elevation in less than a mile. It is not for the faint of heart. There is a reason most athletes aren't huge fans of the Incline. It's a heck of a workout. The Incline is one of the most unique and challenging trails in the country and it attracts people from all over the world.

The Incline is a trail made up of gravel and large railroad ties made of wood. The trail is just over a mile long and it remains a popular workout destination for aspiring Olympic athletes. There reportedly are 2,744 steps on the Incline.

The Manitou Incline was originally built as a cable car to carry materials to build pipelines on Pikes Peak. After the pipelines were finished, it was turned into a tourist attraction to bring guests to the top of the foothills for a spectacular view of Colorado Springs and the eastern plains.

The wrestlers would frequently do workouts at the Incline, typically on Saturday mornings. The coaches would schedule those, in part, so the athletes didn't stay out too late having fun on Friday nights.

If you went out and had too much on Friday night, you would pay dearly for it the next morning at the Incline.

The Incline was anything but fun. It was grueling and torturous. And challenging. It was not an easy workout and it was done at high altitude, making it more difficult to breathe and catch your breath.

Athletes in other sports also did the Incline. Among the elite athletes, Olympic gold medal speedskater Apolo Ohno was the king of the Incline – he had the unofficial record for the fastest time at just under

19 minutes. Olympic gold medalist Henry Cejudo took a run at the record – his best time was around 20 minutes.

A man named Joseph Gray claimed to have done the Incline in what would be a record time of 17 minutes, 45 seconds.

For most of us, it took a lot longer. It was a workout that would test your mettle and it was source of pride for those of us who could do it.

I had another hill of my own to climb in trying to knock off Justin Ruiz.

I entered April's U.S. Open as the No. 2 seed behind Justin. The Open was an important event because the champion would earn an automatic berth into the finals of the Olympic Trials.

The remaining qualifiers would have to go through a challenge tournament before facing the U.S. Open champion in the finals of the Olympic Trials.

I was feeling really confident at that point.

I was disciplined with my diet and I was eating healthy. I wasn't drinking. And I was doing everything right with my training.

I was ready to roll, but I knew early in the tournament that I wouldn't be the guy earning the automatic berth to the finals of the Olympic Trials.

I suffered a first-round upset loss at the 2008 U.S. Open.

I was defeated by Frank Workman.

I wasn't thinking about Frank. I was already looking ahead. And it cost me.

He threw me in a headlock and caught me on my back.

That loss kind of became a blessing in disguise for me.

My first coach, Rob Hermann, approached me after the loss.

"Adam, this is going to be good for you," he said calmly. "You're facing some adversity. You've never had to come back like that."

I didn't think it was good at first, but I learned a lot from that experience. And what Rob was saying made a lot of sense.

I learned that I had to take it one match at a time and not over-look anybody.

Frank Workman was a good wrestler and he had been on the U.S. National Team. But he was a guy I shouldn't have lost to. Especially just a couple of months before the Olympic Trials.

I went behind the bleachers after I lost the match to Frank Workman. I was in tears. I was not happy. I was still pissed as I tried to regroup while wrestling on the backside of the bracket.

I came all the way back to place third, defeating Robby Smith 3-0, 4-0 in my final bout.

I was pretty determined after the loss to Workman. I didn't allow a point after that first-round loss.

Justin Ruiz downed R.C. Johnson in the finals of the U.S. Open. Justin had advanced to the final-round series of the Olympic Trials.

He was now just two wins away from making the 2008 Olympic Team.

The U.S. Open was a tournament that didn't play out the way I had hoped obviously, but I still had another two months to prepare for the Olympic Trials.

I was still upset when the U.S. Open ended.

I was talking to my wife after the loss and my level of frustration was still high.

"Maybe I should just stop now and be done with wrestling," I told her.

"You're not doing that," she said. "You've worked too hard. You can come back from this."

I had all of these negative thoughts in my head. I wasn't really going to quit. I was just venting and I was pissed off that I had lost.

Marley was the most supportive she's ever been. She really encouraged me and tried to help me bounce back from that defeat.

That definitely helped me as I moved forward.

Marley was always there to pick me up when I was down.

I talked to Coach Hermann and he also was supportive. He turned that setback into a positive for me. His words of encouragement were super helpful. I really appreciated him being in the corner. He was the guy who gave me a chance to wrestle for the Navy team when I didn't have any other options after I joined the Coast Guard.

Even with the support I had, the bottom line was I did lose my focus and I did lose a match I shouldn't have lost.

That couldn't happen again.

Overcoming Obstacles to Excel

For the first time in a while, I had to really refocus. I was still confident in my abilities, and after blowing off some steam and calming down, I knew I was on track to make the Olympic Team.

I had two months to prepare for the Olympic Trials and I was going to do everything in my power to prepare to be at my absolute best.

Ivan Ivanov, my coach at the USOEC, would always tell me how explosive I was when I was wrestling.

I remember in 2006, I was at a January training camp in Colorado Springs and I was wrestling against Justin Ruiz in practice. He beat me pretty bad for an hour in a grind match. U.S. National Coach Steve Fraser believed very strongly in those types of matches. It built conditioning and mental toughness.

I had to mentally go to a different place to get through them.

The grind matches would essentially be 60 to 90 minutes of non-stop wrestling. A regular match in competition, was only 6 to 9 minutes. I liked the grind matches and they helped strengthen me mentally and physically.

When we finished for the day, I was down and a little frustrated after having my butt kicked by Justin.

Ivan approached me after practice with some words of encouragement.

"Don't worry, Adam, this isn't how we train. You're an explosive athlete. You will beat him in a real match."

As usual, Ivan was right.

I wrestled Justin a short time later at the Kit Carson Cup.

And I beat him.

It was a close match and it came down to the old clinch rule where both wrestlers started in the body lock position before the whistle blew.

It was a position I worked hard on with training partner R.C. Johnson back at Northern Michigan.

My match with Justin was tied so we went to the clinch.

The referee blew the whistle and I threw Justin belly-to-belly right away to his back and scored the points that I needed.

And I won the match.

BELIEVE AND ACHIEVE

Justin was just coming off winning a bronze medal at the World Championships, but I had beaten him for the first time.

Winning that match built my confidence. It was another stepping-stone for me.

I was really pumped after that win.

Up until that time, he had beaten me seven or eight times.

He had beaten me pretty bad, by technical fall, when we first started wrestling.

Earning that first win over Justin was awesome.

I didn't run around the mat or do a backflip.

I never showed too much emotion on the mat after a big win. I didn't want to show up my opponent.

But that didn't mean I wasn't excited.

Beating Justin was a big step for me.

One of the biggest areas where I improved after I came to the Olympic Training Center in Colorado Springs was with my strength.

I started working with Mike Favre, a strength coach at the OTC. That made a big difference for me.

Mike was awesome for me and his influence made a big impact on me.

He brought a different approach that really worked for me. And it paid off.

I used to do more of a body-building type of strength training, but under Mike I was working less on sculpting my physique and more on building the type of strength that would translate to wrestling.

He was training the athletes to become faster and more explosive with our athletic movements.

We did exercises very specific to wrestling and unique to our sport.

He had us do lifts in which we were jumping over a bar to simulate the reverse lift we did on the mat. It was light weight where you would explode.

We would use old beer kegs, filled with water, and lift them to build power for wrestling techniques.

We had one day called "strong man day" where we could do circuit lifting that was like what cross-fit training is today. Mike was always ahead of the game and on the cutting-edge with many of his philosophies.

He was a well-educated strength coach who knew how to put everything together.

After working with Mike, I was more explosive and able to lift guys off the mat more easily.

I typically lifted weights on Monday, Wednesday and Friday with the rest of the Greco-Roman team. Then I would sneak in there on a Tuesday or a Thursday and do a workout.

I felt like I needed to lift an extra day or do some extra lifts.

I would stay after practice and do extra workouts every day.

I would always do extra work.

We would also do a pummeling workout with dumb bells.

And we had a machine called an arm bike. I would sit down and work my arms in a circular motion like riding a bike.

I would do a lot of extra pullups, at least three times a week.

I would use a 50-pound Bulgarian power bag to build my endurance. I would swing them overheard and then throw them on the floor. I would also do pushups and sit-ups with them.

I was a big 211-pounder. I walked around at about 235 pounds when I was in good shape. And I was a super lean 235, so it was a challenge for me to drop down to 211 for a competition.

The weight class was listed at 96 kilograms with FILA, the international governing body of wrestling. We were the only country to use pounds to measure weight. The rest of the world used the metric system and measured weight in kilograms.

One kilogram equals 2.2 pounds.

I did extra cardio workouts, mainly running, to keep my weight down.

One day a week, I would run a mile and a half. After two practices a day, I would go home and eat dinner. Then I would go run after that to keep my metabolism going.

I also would do a slower-paced three-mile jog.

I did each of those runs once a week.

We also were doing the Incline twice a week.

I felt good. I didn't believe in overtraining. I really pushed myself to my limits.

For me, it worked because I was becoming stronger and better.

I was training at the highest capacity that an athlete could. It was impossible for anyone to do more than I was doing. I really believed that.

I had that mindset that I wanted it so bad that I literally poured everything I had into it.

I was a big believer in training when other people weren't training and when other people weren't watching.

I didn't have an off day. I did Yoga one day a week as an active recovery. I did a basic Yoga at my gym, 24-Hour Fitness. It was a lot of stretching. I think it helped my flexibility and my mobility. It also helped me lift people in wrestling, and it helped me defend against my opponents. Yoga helped my body recover.

I really believed in stretching – I would do that for 15 or 20 minutes after every practice.

I had to be incredibly disciplined.

During that time, I also worked as a part-time personal trainer at 24 Hour Fitness.

I learned about calories and protein as part of my job, and it really helped me personally as an athlete.

I made an Excel spreadsheet and wrote down everything that I ate.

I stayed lighter during 2008 and didn't let my weight go too high after a competition.

For breakfast at the Olympic Training Center, I would eat egg-white vegetable omelets, a small amount of oatmeal and a couple of pieces of fruit. I would see other guys in my weight class eating these huge omelets loaded with all kinds of meat and cheese.

I was bigger than all of the guys in my weight class and I had to be disciplined with everything I ate.

My mindset was to do whatever I had to do to win.

I wanted to gain any type of an edge that I could.

I had to be all-in, 100 percent.

I was counting my food and counting my calories.

I would eat fish and chicken, and Marley would cook for me.

When I was traveling, that was the hardest time because my food options were more limited.

I didn't take a sip of alcohol in 2008. Prior to that, I liked having a couple of beers with my friends. The last beer I had before the June 2008 Olympic Trials was at the World Championships in September 2007.

Marley played a huge role in my preparation. She was 100 percent supportive and made sure I had enough time to devote to my training. And she made sure everything else was taken care of.

This Olympic quest wasn't just for me. It was for us. And Marley was right there with me.

I became laser-focused and stayed the course.

Justin Ruiz had been the No. 1 guy at 96 kilograms for the entire four-year Olympic cycle from 2005-08. He won a World bronze medal in 2005 and he was a member of the 2007 U.S. squad that won the team title at the World Championships.

He had won the 2008 U.S. Open to earn an automatic berth in the Olympic Trials. He was in the driver's seat to represent the U.S. at the 2008 Olympic Games in Beijing, China.

Justin had been in the same position four years before. He won the U.S. Open in 2004 before falling to 2000 Olympic bronze medalist Garrett Lowney in the finals of the 2004 Olympic Trials in Indianapolis.

As motivated as I was to make the Olympic Team in 2008, I knew Justin had plenty of motivation as well after his near-miss in 2004.

When I arrived at UNLV's Thomas and Mack Center in Las Vegas, I knew it was going to be a difficult road to make the 2008 Olympic Team.

The atmosphere for the Olympic Trials was electric with enthusiastic crowds of 6,000 fans for each session. The Trials are a must-see event for wrestling fans that feature tremendous competition with so much at stake.

They take place only once every four years and wrestling in the Olympic Games is the pinnacle for our sport.

There was so much riding on this competition, and many athletes may only have one realistic shot to make an Olympic Team.

BELIEVE AND ACHIEVE

Athletes obviously wanted to be at their peak for this event.

I knew I would face a long, challenging day to reach my goals, but I had trained for it.

I was ready for the Olympic Trials.

I would have to first win three matches in the challenge tournament during the day. I would then have to win two more matches that night in the finals against a guy who would be fresh after sitting out all day.

The entire weight class was wrestling in just one day, so being in peak physical condition was an absolute must for me.

I would have to win five matches against the best guys in the country, but I learned my lesson at the U.S. Open.

I had to take it one match at a time. I couldn't look ahead or I would lose like at the Open.

It would be a daunting task, but it was something I was ready for. I had trained harder than I ever had and I was in the best shape of my life.

Justin Ruiz was sitting out as the U.S. Open champion, so the second- and third-place finishers from the Open would be the top two seeds in the challenge tournament at the Olympic Trials.

The winner of the challenge tournament would then face Justin in the best-of-3 match finals.

My buddy and training partner, R.C. Johnson, had placed second at the U.S. Open so he was the No. 1 seed in the challenge tournament. I had placed third at the Open and would be the 2 seed.

It was going to be difficult just to win the challenge tournament. Our weight class of 96 kilograms/211.5 pounds was deep and loaded with a number of experienced athletes. Many of us had trained and competed against each other for years, so we all knew each other well.

My first match was against Deon Hicks of the U.S. Army. Deon had beaten me at the Armed Forces tournament a few years before. That was the only time we had wrestled in competition.

He was an athletic and dangerous wrestler and I had to be ready.

I came out strong and prevailed 4-2, 5-0 in the quarterfinals.

Next up was a semifinal bout versus Robby Smith, a talented young wrestler who would go on to place fifth in the World in 2015 and make an Olympic Team in 2016.

Robby came out strong and beat me 4-0 in the first period.

He reverse-lifted me into the air right off the whistle and threw me. It was the first period I had ever lost to Robby.

And it definitely got my attention.

I was one period away from losing to Robby and having my dream of making the Olympics come to an abrupt end.

He was a guy who always came at me aggressively.

I had always beaten him when we had wrestled before.

I knew I had the edge in terms of my experience and my ability. I just needed to execute.

My mentality was to come back strong. Robby had just thrown me, but I was still confident.

I knew I would have to fight through some adversity on this day and this was my first taste of it.

I obviously had to score in the second period and win that period against Robby or I was done.

I came right back by hitting an arm drag to a belly-to-belly, body-lock throw. I put some big points on the scoreboard and now I was ready to roll. After that, I had to focus on my defense.

I won the second period 4-1 to force a deciding third period.

Robby fought back and the third period was a battle.

Time was running out in the final period and I had to do something. I felt my hands lock and touch in the final 10 seconds of the match. I was able to score on a lift and beat him 4-0. I pulled that match out in the final seconds.

Walking off the mat, my first thought was, "Holy crap, I almost lost that match to a guy that I had never lost to."

Fortunately, I was able to regroup and advance to the finals of the challenge tournament.

Robby really pushed me, but you have to expect that when you are battling at the Olympic Trials.

Every wrestler's dream is to compete in the Olympic Games.

And crazy things would happen every four years when the Olympic Trials were held and athletes were doing everything in their power to win.

BELIEVE AND ACHIEVE

The win over Robby set me up to face the guy I expected to face.

I would once again face R.C. Johnson, one of the best wrestlers in the country. We were evenly matched, we knew the exact style the other guy wrestled and we were good friends.

Wrestling someone like that is extremely difficult, but I knew he wanted to win just as bad as I did. He wanted to be an Olympian, too.

The matches with R.C. were low-scoring and strategic. This bout unfolded like they usually did when we faced each other. We battled for three periods, but neither one of us could score a takedown or were able to secure a turn.

The scores of the match were 1-1, 1-1, 1-1.

I won a coin flip, so I had won the third and deciding period because I scored last after he was unable to turn me.

He was so strong and powerful. He went to gutwrench me and my whole lower body came off the mat. I was somehow able to stop him. I'm not sure how, but I did.

I breathed another huge sigh of relief.

It was an anxiety-filled match, but I had survived.

It wasn't pretty, but I did what I needed to do.

I hugged R.C. after the match and then he said something to me.

"Now make sure you win," R.C. said, "so I can go to Beijing with you."

"All right buddy, I will take you when I win," I told him.

We had both talked previously about taking the other guy as a training partner to the Olympics if one of us made it.

My mindset going into the Olympic Trials was that this likely was going to be the last tournament of my career.

I had planned on going into a career in law enforcement and would be done wrestling after the 2008 season ended.

I wanted to do everything I possibly could to win. I wanted to give it everything I had and walk away with no regrets.

I wanted to leave everything out on the mat.

Now I was one step – one huge step – away from achieving my goal of becoming a 2008 Olympian.

I had won three tough matches to win the challenge tournament. But none of that mattered now.

I had to win two more matches against Justin Ruiz in the finals to make the Olympic Team.

We had a break between sessions, so I went back to the hotel by myself. I found something to eat, took a nap for an hour and then took a shower.

I stayed focused.

My family and friends were going out to eat between sessions, and in past years I would always join them, but this time was different.

I had to be a little bit selfish and focus on being at my very best for the finals against Justin.

I needed to rest and relax for a few hours, so I could be ready for the biggest matches of my life.

It was a long day, and I needed some recovery time between sessions.

Going into that final-round series, I had earned two wins over Justin in my career, but he had beaten me around 15 times. He also had won a handful of matches in a row over me going into the finals of the Olympic Trials.

One thing I was certain about – Justin Ruiz had beaten me every time it mattered.

It was time for a reversal of fortune.

We had wrestled in the finals of the World Team Trials the year before, but this would be the first time we would square off at the Olympic Trials.

Justin was rested and fresh for the finals because he had been sitting out all day, but I couldn't worry about that. I just had to worry about what I could control.

I knew winning the first match would be pivotal in the series with Justin.

Whoever lost the first match would have to win two straight matches. The pressure on the guy who lost the first match would be enormous.

I had already wrestled three matches that day, so the nerves you might normally have in the first match of a tournament were gone for me. I was relaxed, focused and ready to go.

My level of conditioning was good enough to wrestle a full three matches, but dropping the first match would magnify the pressure on me even more.

Rob Hermann and Neal Rodak were in my corner coaching me during the finals.

I came out strong and I was able to win the first match against Justin. The scores were 2-2, 1-1, 1-1. I was able to turn him with a gut-wrench.

The gut-wrench was something he hadn't seen me do before. I am sure that caught him a little bit by surprise.

And it worked perfectly for me.

I was one win away from landing an Olympic berth.

I made a conscious effort not to celebrate and not be overly happy after that win.

I had scored just my third career win over Justin, but I couldn't get too high after that victory because I knew I had to do it again.

We had about an hour break before the second match.

After I won the first match, I remember the nerves kicked in a little bit more. I think it was maybe because I knew I had only one more win to make the Olympic Team.

I had won the first match, but it was super close.

I just tried to stay professional and keep the same mindset and aggression.

I sat down in a chair in the warmup area and rested as the other matches finished up in the first round.

I fully expected Justin to come back strong and he did. He took the second match by scores of 3-0, 4-0. He was able to turn me with a gut-wrench and he scored a reversal.

Now the nerves were really kicking in.

As I walked out to the mat for the third match against Justin, I heard a voice yell down from the crowd.

"He's not going to give it to you. You have to take it from him."

I recognized that voice. It was my brother, William. And what he yelled was something that stuck with me.

The 2008 U.S. Olympic Greco-Roman berth at 96 kilograms would come down to one final match.

It was the biggest match of my life and I needed to bounce back from the setback in the second match.

Justin struck first in the first period of the final match. He won the opening period by a 2-1 score. He scored a reversal off my move to win the period.

I thought I should have won that period 2-1, but they didn't give me the points I thought I had scored on a reverse headlock.

Now I needed to win the final two periods or he would be headed to Beijing.

I had to keep wrestling tough. Not scoring in that first period didn't affect me.

I was in the best shape of my life and I trusted my conditioning.

I won a strategical second period 1-1 to even the match at one period apiece. Neither of us could secure a turn. I won the coin flip, so I scored last to win the period.

Now it all came down to one final, two-minute period for the Olympic berth.

I wanted to take charge early. I wanted to score on my feet and I nearly scored a takedown from a double-underhook position. I almost spun behind Justin before he turned his hips to stop me from scoring. He was a savvy veteran who wasn't going to give up anything easy.

After a scoreless first minute on our feet, the referee tossed a coin into the air.

The coin hit the mat, rolled a short distance and then came to a stop.

It came up blue, the color of my singlet.

I would be in the top position of the first 30-second segment in par terre and Justin would be on top for the final 30 seconds.

I had the advantage.

I was able to lift Justin near the end of the first 30 seconds and our momentum carried us over near the edge of the mat where I drove him out of bounds for a pushout and scored one point.

That point didn't really mean anything because even if I hadn't scored, he would still need to turn me in the final 30 seconds to win.

Now it all came down to my defense. I had to prevent him from scoring.

Justin was determined to score. Time was running out and he lifted me up off the mat in the final seconds, but I fought him off and he was unable to turn me with a gut-wrench.

The clock ran out and the match ended.

I had landed a spot on the 2008 United States Olympic Greco-Roman Wrestling Team.

I slapped the mat and pumped my right fist as a smile spread across my face. Just a few feet away, Justin was on his knees with his face buried in his hands.

I climbed to my feet and raised both arms in celebration. And then I flexed my arms as my family and friends, and many others in the crowd, gave me a standing ovation.

When the match ended, I saw Justin start crying. He was devastated and heartbroken. I decided not to run around when I won because I had empathy for Justin. It was all kind of surreal. I had my arm raised by the referee and I turned and hugged Justin. I told him, "I'm sorry, Justin. You're the best." I know how much he wanted this as well. He was a great wrestler and a great person who had definitely pushed me and made me elevate my game. He had been the gold standard in our weight class for a number of years.

I immediately walked over to my corner and hugged my coaches, Rob Hermann and Neal Rodak.

Ivan Ivanov was standing just a few feet behind them. Ivan was clapping his hands and smiling. I know that win meant a lot to Ivan – he had a huge impact on me.

As my hand was raised by the official, an announcement was made over the loudspeakers by Sandy Stevens:

"Your 2008 Greco-Roman Olympian at 96 kilograms, Adam Wheeler!"

I experienced a flood of emotions at that point.

Joy, relief, satisfaction, redemption, jubilation.

I had done it.

I accomplished my goal of becoming a United States Olympian.

Moments after the match, the broadcast on NBC flashed to a sign in the stands that read, "This is ADAM's House."

There also were signs in my cheering section that read: "ADAM is the WHEELer deal" and "BIG WHEELS keep turning."

Overcoming Obstacles to Excel

I had a cheering section of family and friends of close to 50 people at the Olympic Trials. Where I grew up in southern California was only a short drive to the Trials in Las Vegas.

The NBC cameras then zoomed in on Marley, who was wearing an "ADAM WHEELER WRESTLING" shirt. She had a huge smile on her face while clapping and then raising her arms over her head. She looked up and saw herself on the video screen. Then she became emotional as reality started to sink in.

It became even more real when I walked off the mat and hugged my coaches before turning my attention to my biggest fan.

I walked into the stands, found my wife and wrapped my arms around her as we embraced.

Marley and I both had huge smiles on our faces as we hugged.

I couldn't have done any of this without my wife's incredible and unwavering support. She had been there with me every step of the way since we started dating at Northern Michigan.

She was a huge part of my journey. She supported me in every way imaginable.

When I won, it was like a victory for both of us.

She went through all of the highs and lows during that time.

She was completely invested into what I was doing.

She was working full-time as a teacher. She was the breadwinner in our house.

When I found Marley in the stands, it was an emotional and incredible moment.

"You did it!" she said.

"I love you, Marley," I said.

I had actually envisioned that moment – running up and hugging my wife after making the Olympic Team.

I remember in 2004 seeing Dennis Hall run up into the stands and hug his wife after he beat Brandon Paulson in an epic match at the Olympic Trials in Indianapolis.

So once my hand was raised, I knew where I was headed.

I knew exactly where my wife was sitting and I started in that direction.

NBC broadcaster Matt Devlin summed it all up shortly after my win.

"He is an Olympian," Devlin told the viewers. "And on this night, Adam Wheeler and his family know the emotions of all the hard work, the dedication and the sacrifice. And Adam Wheeler is headed to Beijing."

After I hugged Marley, I turned to walk over to an area just off the main arena floor to do interviews.

At that point, I heard a familiar voice call out to me.

It was my former Navy teammate, Steven Mays.

I walked over to him and he shook my hand.

"Awesome job, man!" Steven said enthusiastically. "Congratulations!"

He was one of my mentors when I first started wrestling Greco for the Navy team.

Steven was an Olympian, and he was one of the guys I wanted to emulate.

I had a blood rag that I would keep under my singlet that Steven had given me years before.

I pulled the rag out and showed it to him, and I know he became emotional and it put a smile on his face.

It was pretty awesome to have him there.

As you might imagine, it was an incredibly emotional moment for me. I was elated and ecstatic. It was satisfying and fulfilling to know that all of my hard work had finally paid off.

I had endured plenty of setbacks, and second-place finishes, before finally breaking through.

We put so much time, effort and sacrifice into a grueling sport. That's why the wins are so sweet and the losses are so painful.

Wrestling is the toughest sport there is, bar none.

After the finals, I had to stick around the arena to undergo the mandatory drug testing with the U.S. Anti-Doping Agency.

The USADA guy initially wanted to stop me when I was headed into the stands to hug my wife because he had to stay with me the whole time.

But nobody was going to stop me from going up to hug Marley.

I remember my mom ran up to me after I won and said, "You did it, you did it! I'm so proud of you!"

My mom had always been there, through a lot of difficult times over a lot of years, so it was neat to be able to share that moment with each other.

We had overcome more than our share of adversity.

It was really awesome to have Rob Hermann as my coach. He was the coach with the Gator Wrestling Club and the guy who helped launch my career in Greco-Roman wrestling at the Senior level. He was such an integral and influential part of my career. Without him, none of this would have been possible.

Rob is the best corner coach that I had. He was the best tactical coach I had. He gave me pointers during my matches that really helped, and he did so in those matches against Justin.

Neal Rodak was also in my corner. He had a big influence on me. He was a teammate and roommate of mine on the Navy team. My third year on the Navy team was Neal's first year on the Navy team. He had already gone through college and was six years older than me. Neal was a very good wrestler who was No. 4 in the country.

Rob Hermann and I introduced Neal to my wife's twin sister, Emily. Neal then became my brother-in law when he married Emily.

Neal is a lawyer who is now a lieutenant colonel in the Air National Guard.

I still had to spend some time at the arena before I could join my family and friends to celebrate after making the Olympic Team.

Right after the match, I spent about 10 minutes being interviewed by the media.

They kept asking me how I was able to knock off a favored wrestler to make the team.

"I believed I could do it and I trained really hard for this," I told the media. "You can achieve anything if you set your mind to it."

My mental approach was what lifted me to new heights in wrestling. I became mentally strong and had the confidence that I could beat anybody.

Once the competition ended, the entire 2008 U.S. Olympic Team gathered and we were introduced to the fans who had just watched us compete.

BELIEVE AND ACHIEVE

I was one of six Olympians in Greco-Roman wrestling. I would be joined on the American team by Spenser Mango, Jake Deitchler, T.C. Dantzler, Brad Vering and Dremiel Byers.

The members of the U.S. Olympic Team in men's and women's freestyle wrestling were also introduced.

We posed for group photos in Team USA warmups while each holding a small American flag.

It was starting to hit me that I was an Olympian.

And it was an awesome feeling.

It was overwhelming.

Once I finished at drug testing, I could finally leave the venue.

It had been a long day, but an incredibly fulfilling day.

The entire process after I was done wrestling had taken a while, so when I walked outside the arena everybody was gone.

I had to hitch a ride back to the hotel with Brian Gomez, a reporter from the *Colorado Springs Gazette.*

Then the celebration began.

I spent the night hanging out with my family and friends in Las Vegas.

We went to Margaritaville to celebrate.

There were a ton of people there ready for me to hang out with them.

We were able to unwind and drink a few beers. That was the first time I had drank a beer in nearly a year.

We spent time gambling at the casino, but I was exhausted and didn't stay out too late. I was up until around midnight before going to bed.

I woke up in the middle of the night and I was in pain. I was sick to my stomach and I began throwing up.

I had food poisoning. I wasn't sure what it was, but I felt awful.

I tried to sleep in a little bit. Luckily, being sick didn't last for very long.

Even though I didn't feel 100 percent, I woke up that next morning with a smile on my face.

I woke up as an Olympian.

I would be representing the United States at the 2008 Olympic

Games, an event that was set to kick off on August 8, 2008 in Beijing, China.

The Opening Ceremonies were scheduled for 8-8-08 at 8:08 p.m.

I loved the sound of that.

As soon as I accomplished my goal of becoming an Olympian, I knew I immediately had to set a new goal.

And that was to become an Olympic gold medalist.

I knew that was a realistic goal, and I needed to get back on the mat.

There was more work to be done.

BELIEVE AND ACHIEVE

The 2008 U.S. Greco-Roman Olympic Team. From left: Spenser Mango, Joe Betterman, Jake Deitchler, T.C. Dantzler, Brad Vering, Adam Wheeler, Dremiel Byers.

Above: Being introduced to the crowd with the rest of the Olympic Team.

Left: Reacting after earning a tough victory over 2005 World medalist Justin Ruiz to make the 2008 Olympic Team.

Overcoming Obstacles to Excel

Realizing my dream at the Olympic Trials in Las Vegas.

Above: Locking up during a physical battle against rival and friend R.C. Johnson.

Left: In the corner with coaches Momir Petkovic and Rob Hermann.

BELIEVE AND ACHIEVE

Fighting for position in the best-of-3 finals.

I worked hard on my double-underhook as you can see in my battle against Justin.

Overcoming Obstacles to Excel

Left: Looking for an advantage in the finals of the Trials.

Below: Taking control in my first of five wins during a grueling day at the Trials.

Left: My gut-wrench defense was key in my three matches against Justin.

BELIEVE AND ACHIEVE

Left: Coach Rob Hermann had a huge impact on my career.

Below: Battling a strong opponent in Deon Hicks in my first match at the Trials.

Left: Locking up and looking for points in the championship series against Justin Ruiz.

I won a tough battle against R.C. Johnson to win the challenge tournament at the Olympic Trials.

I bounced back to win the 2008 Olympic Trials after placing third earlier that year in the U.S. Open.

BELIEVE AND ACHIEVE

The extra workouts I did paid dividends during a grueling day where I wrestled six tough matches at the Trials.

The memorable moment I officially became an Olympian. It was indescribable.

Overcoming Obstacles to Excel

Above: I didn't celebrate too much after the win, but I definitely enjoyed my big moment in Las Vegas.

Right: I had come a long way since going 1-15 in my first year of wrestling as a high school freshman.

Left: An emotional moment with 2005 World bronze medalist Justin Ruiz at the 2008 Olympic Trials. Justin was a great competitor and a guy who drove me to be my best.

BELIEVE AND ACHIEVE

The best part of my day was hugging my wife, Marley, after I made the Olympic Team. There was no way I could've done that without her incredible support.

I had planned to hug my wife if I won the Trials and it was awesome to have it happen.

Looking for points during my last match at the Trials.

Overcoming Obstacles to Excel

Celebrating with Marley after we realized one of our dreams.

RIght: Mugging for the camera with my old Northern Michigan crew that includes coaches Ivan Ivanov and Jim Gruenwald along with wrestlers Joe Betterman and Spenser Mango.

My cheering section showing their support in Las Vegas. Their support was awesome at the Olympic Trials and again at the Olympics.

BELIEVE AND ACHIEVE

Posing for a photo with President George W. Bush prior to the Opening Ceremonies of the Olympics.

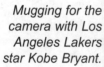

Mugging for the camera with Los Angeles Lakers star Kobe Bryant.

Looking sharp in my Team USA uniform before the Opening Ceremonies.

Our Greco-Roman crew was ready for a big night as the Olympics kicked off on 8-8-08 in Beijing.

BELIEVE AND ACHIEVE

My cheering section of family and friends made a huge difference for me at the Olympics.

Hanging out at practice with the legendary Momir Petkovic, an Olympic gold medalist who played an important role as one of my coaches.

Receiving instructions from Coach Ivan Ivanov at the Olympic Games.

Overcoming Obstacles to Excel

*NBC cameras capture a moment with me and
Coach Momir Petkovic at the Olympics.*

*I was fortunate to have two of the best coaches in the
World in my corner with Momir and Ivan.*

BELIEVE AND ACHIEVE

A break in the action during my Olympic run in Beijing.

Stepping on the mat for the biggest day of my wrestling career.

Overcoming a rough start to prevail and advance at the Olympics.

Overcoming Obstacles to Excel

Pushing the pace in my push toward Olympic bronze.

My defense helped me down the Korean in the bronze-medal match.

BELIEVE AND ACHIEVE

Trying to turn Germany's Mirko Englich in the Olympic semifinals. This was a match I wanted to have back.

Looking for points in the semifinal battle with Mirko.

Staying in good position was a big key for me during my matches at the Olympics.

Setting up a reverse lock during an Olympic matchup.

BELIEVE AND ACHIEVE

2008 Olympic medalists at 96 kg. From left: Silver medalist Mirko Englich of Germany, Gold medalist Aslanbek Khushtov of Russia, Bronze medalist Adam Wheeler of USA and Bronze medalist Asset Mambetov of Kazakhstan.

Stepping on the podium on the biggest day of my wrestling career.

The awards ceremony at the Olympic Games was surreal. It was an amazing experience.

Posing for photographers after the medal ceremony. I won a medal and a nice bouquet of red roses.

Standing on the podium after I was awarded my Olympic bronze medal.

BELIEVE AND ACHIEVE

I found a new competitive outlet when I started training in Jiu Jitsu after my wrestling career ended.

Left: I won the No GI World title in Jiu Jitsu in 2014.

Overcoming Obstacles to Excel

I realized another dream when I became a member of the SWAT team in Colorado Springs.

I look like I could've landed a part in one of the Terminator movies.

Enjoying some family time with my wife, Marley, and our two boys, Jameson and Cal.

BELIEVE AND ACHIEVE

Following in their father's footsteps.

With the love of my life, my wife Marley. Without her amazing support, none of what I accomplished would have been possible.

I was humbled and honored to be inducted into the California Wrestling Hall of Fame in 2018.

CHAPTER 5
Olympic Bronze in Beijing

T he U.S. won the Greco-Roman World team title in 2007, and I had gained valuable experience as a training partner in Baku. I carried that momentum into the 2008 Olympic year with a breakthrough season.

After I knocked off Justin Ruiz to win the 2008 U.S. Olympic Team Trials, I had virtually no media coverage from where I grew up in California. The *Colorado Springs Gazette* did a story on me because I was training in the Springs.

But that was about it.

I really wasn't concerned about how much attention the media was giving me or worried about how much coverage I received.

I had the opportunity of my lifetime coming up.

And I wanted to take full advantage of it.

My win over Justin Ruiz was considered an upset, but I knew I belonged on the Olympic Team.

I beat a World bronze medalist to make the U.S. team and I had beaten Olympic qualifiers from other countries. I felt like I was going to win the Olympics – I didn't have a doubt in my mind. I believed I had hit my peak and I was very, very confident.

I had two months to prepare for the biggest tournament of my life.

I made the Olympic Team on June 15 and I was scheduled to compete at the Olympic Games on August 14 in Beijing, China.

BELIEVE AND ACHIEVE

I had a very short window to prepare for the Olympics, but I absolutely wanted to make the most of that time.

I still had plenty of room to improve. And I also knew that I needed to keep progressing if I was going to reach my goals in Beijing.

I improved dramatically in those two months between the Trials and the Olympics.

I was an Olympian, so the focus was on me and the other five guys who made the Olympic Team in Greco-Roman wrestling.

I had so much attention paid to me by our coaches to help prepare me. I was the guy at 96 kilos, and it was their job to make sure I was prepared for a great performance.

And my coaches did exactly that.

I was working with our three national coaches – Steve Fraser, Momir Petkovic and Anatoly Petrosyan.

I also had Rob Hermann and Ivan Ivanov, my first two Greco coaches, working with me.

I was in good hands with experienced, proven and driven coaches guiding and preparing me for the biggest tournament of my life.

R.C. Johnson and Russ Davie were the two guys I trained with the most.

Russ was a heavyweight and training with him helped me a lot. Russ had a really good gut-wrench and it was more powerful than anybody in my weight class. He was bigger, taller and stronger than me.

After I wrestled Russ, the guys in my weight class felt small. Working with him helped me immensely.

If I could gut-wrench Russ Davie, I knew I could turn anybody in my weight class. And I could turn Russ.

We were pretty evenly matched even though he was a weight class above me. I wrestled him one time in a competition at heavyweight and I won.

But most of the time in practices I was the nail and not the hammer against him. Russ really pushed me and he played a key role in my progression in 2008.

As we moved closer to the competition in Beijing, I trained more with R.C. Johnson. He was the best training partner I could have asked for. And he was in the same weight class as me.

He did everything for me. It didn't matter what I needed, he was there.

He was at every single practice.

The key to being a good partner is being selfless.

R.C. and I both had the same goal before the Olympic Trials. We wanted to make the Olympic Team.

I had defeated R.C. in a close match that could have easily gone the other way at the Olympic Trials. But he put all of that aside to assist me in my preparation for Beijing.

Once I became the Olympian, R.C. showed that selflessness and he was 100 percent committed to helping me. I'm not sure many people would have done that.

We had an interesting dynamic at 96 kilograms.

We competed against each other, but we were also friends off the mat.

We would all sit by each other when we ate lunch in the cafeteria at the Olympic Training Center. I think we had a mutual respect for one another as wrestlers and for how hard we trained. We all lived a similar lifestyle.

When I got married the year before, in 2007, a number of guys in my weight class were in attendance. That group included Justin Ruiz, R.C. Johnson, Robby Smith and Justin Millard.

Brad Vering and Russ Davie were guys I also trained with that were at my wedding. Brad was a weight class below me, but he was a great workout partner. And a really good dude.

R.C. was really there for me as a training partner for the two months leading up to the Olympics.

If I needed to work on a technique, he was there to work with me.

R.C. and I had made each other better from the time I arrived at Northern Michigan in 2003.

I was fortunate to have a guy like that to train with and compete against.

During our pre-Olympic workouts, R.C. was one of the guys challenging me when we had a grueling segment of practice that the coaches called "Shark Bait."

I would stand in the middle of the mat and five other guys in my group would alternate wrestling against me.

Among the guys in my group were James Johnson, R.C. Johnson, Russ Davie and Robby Smith.

I would wrestle against a guy for a minute and then a fresh guy would come in and wrestle me.

Their goal was to come in as hard as they could and push me.

It was a hell of a workout. It was one of the toughest things I remember doing.

They were trying to test me physically and mentally. And trying to break me.

I kept fighting the whole time, but after a short time they started taking it to me and kicking my butt as I became more and more fatigued.

I went 100 percent the whole time, no matter how bad I was doing. I could barely raise my arms because I was so spent near the end of the workout.

But there was no way I was going to quit.

It was a conditioning workout and it was a mental toughness workout.

I was so exhausted after practice that I could barely stand up.

I was one of the few Olympians that finished the practice.

After surviving that workout, I knew there was no way one guy could make me tired.

James Johnson was one of the guys who wrestled with me that day. He was another veteran coach who worked with me before the Olympics.

J.J. was the Greco-Roman coach for the Sunkist Kids Wrestling Club. He was very hands-on with his approach and he would try to help me as much as he could. He had wrestled in my weight class when he competed, so he had some good insights and advice for an upper-weight wrestler.

J.J. was a positive influence who provided a lot of encouragement.

All of the Greco-Roman coaches offered helpful input. I was a sponge during my training, trying to absorb everything I could that might give me an advantage.

Overcoming Obstacles to Excel

It was the most beneficial two months of training I had in my career.

My mindset was completely focused on my preparation for the Olympic Games.

All I did was eat, sleep and breathe wrestling.

When I wasn't training, I was watching DVDs and video of the guys in my weight class who had qualified for the Olympics.

It was a 20-man bracket, so I was trying to learn as much as I could about the other 19 guys at 96 kilograms.

I wanted to learn their go-to move, and I studied how they set it up and executed it.

It didn't necessarily mean I would be able to stop their moves in a match, but I wanted to prepare for them.

I already knew a lot of the guys in my bracket from watching them compete. I had seen a number of them wrestle at the 2007 World Championships. I had a pretty good idea of what moves they liked.

I knew Mirko Englich of Germany had an effective front headlock. I knew him pretty well and I was confident I could beat him.

I also knew the Korean was really strong defensively. I remember him winning a lot of matches because he kept winning the coin flip. He would hold his ground in par terre and not get turned.

That was a big part of the game.

Of the 19 guys I could potentially face in Beijing, I had wrestled eight guys in the bracket.

I felt like it was an advantage that I had faced a few of the guys in my bracket.

I doubt that I was on the radar of a lot of the other guys because I had never wrestled in the World Championships or the Olympic Games.

I wasn't the No. 1 guy in the U.S. and I hadn't made a Senior-level team before.

I think they may have been discounting me.

Justin Ruiz had wrestled for the United States at the last three World Championships.

Justin was a World medalist and he was the guy they expected to see and were paying attention to.

BELIEVE AND ACHIEVE

I think that was an advantage for me because maybe they weren't taking me as seriously as they should have.

My opponents may not have been quite as familiar with my style of wrestling either.

During my preparation for the Olympics, my main area of emphasis was my par terre defense from the down position. If I could stop my opponents from turning me, I had an excellent chance of winning.

The old football mantra of defense wins championships applied to Greco-Roman wrestling.

That area was paramount with so much emphasis being placed on par terre.

If a wrestler won a coin flip, and neither wrestler could score a turn, a wrestler would win the match because he scored last after not being turned from the bottom position.

The rules were a little confusing, especially for someone new to wrestling.

I also worked on my double-underhook position on my feet. I was very close to scoring a takedown against Justin Ruiz at the Olympic Trials with that technique. I worked on double-unders every day in practice. I knew if I got in that position – where a wrestler gains leverage by putting his arms under his opponent's arms – that I was going to score.

I was in excellent shape going into the Trials and I continued to improve on my conditioning after I made the Olympic Team.

I had already been pushing myself before the Olympic Trials and there really wasn't much more that I could do to elevate conditioning.

But the biggest event of my life was approaching and I was constantly looking for an edge. There was no room for slacking. It put me in a different mindset, knowing the Olympic Games were coming up and I was the Olympian.

I was working even harder in practice and I was pushing myself even more in the extra workouts that I did after practice.

I obviously wanted to maximize this opportunity.

My mental focus was even sharper.

I also knew that this was going to be the last competition of my career.

I was set on going to the police academy after the Olympics and pursuing a career in law enforcement.

This was going to be my first and last opportunity to compete in the Olympic Games.

Nobody was picking me to win in Beijing and I wasn't considered among the favorites. But that was fine with me.

There were some very good wrestlers in our weight class, but there weren't any superstars like there were in other divisions like heavyweight with Mijain Lopez of Cuba.

There were plenty of guys, including me, who had a shot at winning the 2008 Olympic gold medal at 211.5 pounds.

In fact, none of the four World medalists from 2007 would win an Olympic medal in 2008.

Part of the reason was the wrestlers were so evenly matched. Another reason was because the coin flip and ball draw seemingly gave everyone a chance to win.

The rules leveled the playing field.

I was one of those guys looking to score takedowns and turn my opponents.

I wasn't waiting to see if I won a coin flip.

That wasn't my mentality or the mentality of the United States team. We wanted to wrestle aggressively, push the pace, impose our will and break our opponents.

But at the same time, we knew we had to be technical and tactical, wrestle smart and not make mistakes.

I believed I had a legitimate shot at winning a gold medal at the 2008 Olympic Games.

The U.S. team was preparing to travel to China and I was ready to go.

I had been training hard for nearly two months in Colorado Springs and most of the hard work was behind me.

I had been to more than 20 countries and some of them numerous times to compete in wrestling. I had also been to the World Championships in 2007, but it was a wrestling-only competition. The Olympic Games were different – they were the pinnacle. They obvi-

BELIEVE AND ACHIEVE

ously were a much bigger event with thousands of athletes in numerous sports converging on Beijing for the most prestigious athletic competition on the planet.

It was difficult to quantify the magnitude of the Olympic Games until we walked into a sold-out, 100,000-seat stadium with the athletes from all of the countries for the Opening Ceremonies.

It was a massive global event.

The Greco-Roman team was the first U.S. wrestling squad to compete at the Olympics, so were the first group to arrive in Beijing on July 30, 2008.

It was another long trip to a place halfway across the world, but I couldn't wait to get there.

We boarded a United Airlines flight for the first leg of the trip. We flew three hours from Colorado Springs to San Francisco. We spent a day there for processing with the U.S. Olympic Committee.

We had a meeting with the USOC about how to conduct ourselves, we took team photos and we received all of our Team USA gear to wear at the Olympics.

It was ridiculous how much clothing we received from Nike and Ralph Lauren, the outfitters for the American team in Beijing.

I met soccer star Brandy Chastain, who scored the dramatic winning goal at the World Cup. I posed for a photo with her and that was cool.

Our team leader, John Bardis, also gave every member of the Olympic Team in Greco a video camera. John really took care of us.

After a day in California, we boarded another plane for a 13-hour flight from San Francisco to Beijing, China.

We would fly across the Pacific Ocean to the north of Hawaii and then over Japan before landing in northern China.

There was a ton of time to kill during the flight.

There was a huge selection of movies and I spent a majority of my time watching a handful of movies I ordered from my seat.

I was sitting next to one of the Olympic women's volleyball players and we talked briefly during the flight. We were both eager and anxious to arrive in China to compete.

I was also able to take a nap.

Overcoming Obstacles to Excel

The flight was long, but it was the best flight that I had ever been on. I could feel a sense of pride throughout the plane. We had athletes from a lot of different sports on our flight, and it was great to meet some of them. The flight actually seemed to go by pretty fast, even though we were in the air for 13 hours.

A new airport had been built in Beijing for the Olympic Games, and it was massive. I was exhausted when we landed. There was a huge time difference between China and Colorado. Beijing was 14 hours ahead of the Mountain time zone and it took a day or two for us to adjust.

When we landed, everything was very structured and organized, and we were able to make it through all the security procedures relatively quickly.

When we walked out of the customs area, there was a huge group of photographers taking pictures of the athletes. We felt like rock stars for a brief moment. We grabbed our luggage and finally made it to the bus before we headed to the Olympic Village. The whole way to the Village, we saw thousands of Olympic flags and signs. It was awesome.

I was loving every minute of it.

Beijing is an enormous city with a population of nearly 20 million people. It is twice the size of New York City.

Beijing is the second most populous city in the world with Shanghai, China ranked No. 1.

Beijing is a large industrial city with more than its share of pollution.

During the Olympics, only half of the vehicles were allowed on the roads by the Chinese government. Cars with even-numbered license plates could be on the road one day with the odd-numbered plates on the road the following day.

Even with the restrictions, the smog was still thick and heavy in Beijing. The air quality was not the best.

It is one of the oldest cities in the world with a rich history. The Great Wall of China, one of the seven wonders of the world, is located a short drive from Beijing.

We had the opportunity to visit the Great Wall during one of the first days we were in China.

2000 Olympic gold medalist Rulon Gardner, working as a broadcaster for NBC, accompanied us on a bus trip to the Great Wall.

Sports Illustrated photographer John McDonough captured an awesome photo of Rulon wrestling with fellow Olympic heavyweight Dremiel Byers on the Great Wall the day before the Opening Ceremonies. Team Leader John Bardis also made it into the photo.

The Great Wall was impressive and massive – I thought it was awesome. It was a huge part of history. It was a super fun day. We had a great group of guys on our Greco team and we enjoyed our visit to the Great Wall.

It was extremely hot and humid, like most of the days we were China.

Rulon was prepared for the warm day. He had packed on a few pounds after he retired as a heavyweight wrestler. He brought a duffel bag with him to the Great Wall that day. He would sweat through a polo shirt and then dip into his bag and put on a dry shirt. He went through about five shirts during the few hours we were at the Great Wall.

I knew Rulon had to be hot because we were all hot and sweaty.

We had a blast that day and that trip was a nice getaway. And it was a good break from our training.

After the sightseeing was done, we had to go back down the hill before boarding the bus back into Beijing.

We each had tiny go-karts that we drove down the hill. We were always competing in something, so it became a race as we tried to beat each other back down to the bottom. It was an enjoyable day with a fun group of guys. We had great camaraderie on our team and we genuinely liked being around each other. That makes a big difference in a demanding, grueling sport like wrestling.

Having a guy like John Bardis around also was inspiring.

John is a former wrestler who had become hugely successful in the business world. He is a millionaire, but you would never know it if you talked to him.

John is one of the most down-to-earth people I have ever met. He is just a very genuine, nice and caring person with a huge heart.

Overcoming Obstacles to Excel

John was the U.S. Team Leader at the World Championships in 2007 and again for the Olympic Team in 2008.

The team leader played an important role. John definitely provided us with financial support, but he did almost everything for us.

He took us out to dinner and provided us with whatever we needed in training.

John would even sit in the sauna with us to help us make weight.

After having a couple of conversations with John, I realized that he may be the smartest person that I know. He is very knowledgeable about so many topics.

One day in Beijing, John took us shopping. He took the Olympians to a shop where a tailor took our measurements and made suits for us.

Olympic teammates Dremiel Byers, T.C. Dantzler and Jake Deitchler went as well.

It was an awesome experience and John was an incredibly generous man. I was very grateful for everything he did for me.

Shortly after we arrived in Beijing, the six-man American Greco-Roman wrestling team did a press conference at the Main Press Center. We were all seated together while facing the media with our names on placards in front of us. We also had microphones in front of each of us to answer questions.

We were competing in the early part of the Olympics, so we were one of the first teams to do a press conference.

A U.S. Olympic Committee official informed us that the press conference before us was a little dry and boring. He joked that maybe we could generate a little more enthusiasm and excitement when we met with the media.

That wasn't a problem for our group. We embraced the opportunity to have some fun in our meeting with the media.

We were in a massive room that seated several hundred media members. It wasn't quite full, but we had a good number of media members there.

I was on a U.S. Olympic Greco-Roman Team with a number of wrestlers with impressive credentials.

Dremiel Byers was a World champion and a World bronze

medalist. Brad Vering had just won a World silver medal in 2007. Spenser Mango was a World University champion and Junior World medalist. T.C. Dantzler was a member of the 2007 team that won the title at the World Championships.

Spenser and I were teammates at Northern Michigan, and he's just a down-to-earth, good dude. It was fun being teammates with him on the Olympic Team.

Dremiel told a funny story about wrestling in Cuba and the always charismatic T.C. had the media laughing as well. We had some big personalities on our team and the USOC official was loving the energy our guys brought to the room.

We also had 18-year-old Jake Deitchler on the team. Jake had earned a ton of media attention after knocking off two-time World bronze medalist Harry Lester to make our team. Jake had just finished high school and his story had resonated with media across the country. His story even made it into *Sports Illustrated.*

Jake was a good kid and he received more media attention before Beijing than the rest of the Greco team combined.

Jake was young and inexperienced. It was very cool that he pulled off a huge upset at the Olympic Trials and he had earned his spot on the team.

2006 World champion Joe Warren was expected to be the seventh member of our team, but he had been suspended after failing a drug test and he wasn't eligible to make the Olympic Team in 2008. The U.S. fell short of qualifying for the Olympics in his weight class of 60 kilograms. I wish we had qualified at that weight because another friend and college teammate, Joe Betterman, would have been a great addition to our team.

Joe was a member of the American team that won the World Championships in 2007. He won the Olympic Trials in 2008, but wasn't able to compete at the Olympics because we hadn't qualified in his weight class.

And then there was me. I had made a University World Team and wrestled in the World Cup twice. But I had never made a World or Olympic team on the Senior level until now. Not many people had heard much about me or were even aware of who I was.

Overcoming Obstacles to Excel

The press conference started and the media asked a number of questions. Our coach, Steve Fraser, also was seated with us along with USA Wrestling communications director Gary Abbott.

Every U.S. wrestler except me was asked a question during the formal part of the press conference. I just sat there and listened to their responses.

I still managed to have a good time during the press conference because our guys did a good job and they were joking around and telling funny stories.

They were very engaging and the media picked up on that.

I was sitting in between two of our leaders, Brad Vering and Dremiel Byers, and they both answered a number of questions. They were veteran guys who had won World medals.

Not being asked any questions gave me even more incentive to want to do well at the Olympics. I remember talking to Coach Fraser after that press conference.

Fraser knew I wasn't asked any questions.

"Don't worry about it, Adam," he said. "It's fine."

"That's OK," I replied. "They will want to talk to me when I'm done."

"Yes, they will," he said with a smile.

Fraser was a 1984 Olympic champion who was the long-time U.S. National Coach for Greco-Roman wrestling.

Finally, after the formal part of the press conference ended, a reporter came up to ask me a question.

"Hi Adam, I hear you went to college with Spenser Mango. What do you think about his chances in the tournament?" the reporter asked.

"I think Spenser has a chance to do really well," I said. "He's a talented young wrestler with a bright future ahead. I think he can win a medal."

It turned out the reporter was from Spenser's hometown of St. Louis. I didn't mind helping the guy with a story about Spenser.

After we arrived in Beijing in late July, we would have two weeks of training to prepare and get down to weight for the competition.

The U.S. teams in most of the sports were training at Beijing Normal University, a college with a massive athletic training facility.

BELIEVE AND ACHIEVE

It was located right in the heart of the city.

They had a good-sized, wrestling room for us at BNU that had three full-sized mats. We also had a sauna. And they had an outdoor stadium with a grass field and a running track around it.

We spent one evening playing soccer at the stadium for a cross-training workout. The heat was stifling that night, and with all of the running we did while chasing around a soccer ball, it ended up being a grueling workout.

The teams were split up, and it was the old guys vs. the young guys. I was on the young guys team, but unfortunately, the old guys beat us 2-0.

I didn't score any goals. It turned out the best player on the field was our strength coach, Mike Favre. Mike scored the only two goals of the night. The best part of the soccer game for me was it provided me with another chance to build my stamina as we moved closer to the wrestling competition.

The buildings at the college were older, but it was still a good facility where we did our final training leading up to the competition.

They also had dorms and a huge cafeteria at Beijing Normal and that is where the training partners stayed.

Right across the hall from the wrestling room at BNU was a large pool where the U.S. Olympic swimmers were training prior to the Games.

Among the swimmers training next door to us was Michael Phelps, who would go on to win a record eight Olympic gold medals in Beijing.

The USA basketball team, made up entirely of NBA stars, also practiced on a court at Beijing Normal.

My weight was in good shape when we arrived in China. I was weighing right around 230 pounds, which put me in good shape to comfortably make it down to my weight class of 211.5 for the Olympics.

We had two weeks to train and acclimate. Most of the hard training was already done before we left Colorado.

We still had tough practices in Beijing, but the hardest part was behind us when we arrived in China.

Overcoming Obstacles to Excel

We stayed at the Olympic Village and it was an unbelievable place. It was beautiful. I loved it there.

The accommodations were great, the food was excellent and everything was first-class all the way.

The atmosphere in the Village was amazing with some of the greatest athletes in the world in every Olympic sport staying in the same place.

I was rooming with Brad Vering, who had made his second straight Olympic Team.

Brad was the best guy I could have roomed with.

He had been to an Olympic Games and he knew what to expect.

He was our informal team captain and was a great leader. Everybody respected Brad. He led vocally and by example. He had just won a World silver medal the year before. Brad was a guy many of us really looked up to. He was hard worker and a tough competitor. And a damn good wrestler.

I felt like he shared my similar focus.

We were there to work out, train and be ready to compete. We wanted to make sure we didn't get too distracted with everything else going on at the Olympics.

We were cutting weight, but we still had to eat.

The cafeteria at the Olympic Village was awesome. It had everything we needed.

It had different types of foods and cuisines for people coming there from all around the world.

They had healthy food and a lot to choose from.

I was eating clean at the time. It was a great set-up, especially for the athletes in combat sports who were managing their weight.

Going to the cafeteria at the Village was interesting because I saw athletes not only from different countries, but also from different sports.

I saw 100-pound gymnasts and 300-pound weightlifters. There were athletes of all shapes and sizes in Beijing.

I maintained a strict diet during my time leading up to competition. I had to be disciplined or I wouldn't make weight.

Most of my meals would include chicken breast and different

types of vegetables. I ate a lot of veggies to keep my stomach full.

I snacked on tomatoes and cucumbers. They were relatively low in calories and would keep me satisfied.

I had a protein shake before my morning workout. And then I would eat a veggie egg-white omelet, oatmeal and fruit for breakfast after my workout.

I would snack on tuna and eat apples around lunchtime. And have another protein shake.

Following our afternoon practice, I would have fish and chicken for dinner.

I had a post-recovery workout shake with protein and carbs in it.

I was very disciplined and regimented with everything I did, especially my diet.

I was dropping a significant amount of weight and I needed to be smart about what I ate to stay healthy and maintain my strength.

I had a routine and I stuck with it.

They also had a McDonald's at the Olympic Village and one next to the college where we trained. But I stayed away. I like McDonald's, but I couldn't put that kind of food into my body at that point. No Big Mac's for me.

I grabbed a Snickers bar and took it with me every day when I left the cafeteria, but I couldn't eat them because I was cutting weight.

I was saving them all so I could eat them after the competition.

Brad Vering, my roommate, made fun of me because I had 12 full-sized Snickers bars in my room before I competed.

After the Olympics, I ate one of the Snickers bars and then decided I wasn't going to pack them for the trip home. I gave them away.

I spent a lot of time in the sauna. They had a sauna at Beijing Normal and at the gym at the Olympic Village.

Sitting in the sauna was so relaxing for me. Plus, it would help me cut the remaining pounds I had to lose to make weight.

The competition was closing in fast and that really hit home when we took part in the Opening Ceremonies on August 8, 2008.

There were 16 U.S. wrestlers – six in Greco-Roman, six in men's freestyle and four in women's freestyle – who had qualified for the Olympic Team.

Overcoming Obstacles to Excel

We were all invited to take part in the Opening Ceremonies.

Everyone decided to go except Brad Vering, who took part in the 2004 Opening Ceremonies in Athens, Greece after he made his first Olympic Team in Greco.

Brad was coming off a silver medal finish at the 2007 World Championships and was one of the favorites to win an Olympic gold medal at his weight class of 84 kilograms/185 pounds.

Like me, Brad was completely focused on doing everything he could to make sure he was ready to give his best performance in Beijing.

He knew the Opening Ceremonies were going to be an extremely long night, so he decided to skip it and make sure he got enough sleep that night.

I thought about doing that as well, but I ultimately decided to go.

I was still six days away from my competition on the 14th.

Going to the Opening Ceremonies wasn't going to make or break me.

I am glad that I took part in it.

The U.S. Olympic athletes in all of the sports boarded buses at the Olympic Village and were taken to the fencing venue.

We walked into the venue and the only athletes in there were Americans.

A short time after we arrived, an announcement was made.

"Please welcome President George W. Bush and former President George H.W. Bush."

The two Bushes walked out side-by-side to loud cheers from the American athletes.

That was pretty exciting and really neat to see.

We were halfway around the world and the most powerful man on the planet was standing in the same room with us.

The President of the United States and the former President were there to greet us and wish us luck. They were both huge sports fans who were big supporters of the Olympic Games.

President Bush delivered a short speech and then he and his father walked around to meet as many athletes as they could.

They shook hands and posed for photos with teams in each sport.

BELIEVE AND ACHIEVE

President Bush posed for a photo with the 15 American wrestlers who were there that night.

I was able to shake hands with the current President and I posed for a photo in which I was next to and just slightly behind George W. Bush.

We also spoke briefly that night.

"You ready, big guy?" the President asked me with a smile.

"Yes, Sir!" I responded.

That was a memorable moment for me.

After we left the fencing venue, we walked a short distance to the gymnastics venue. Athletes from all of the countries were in there as the Opening Ceremonies kicked off.

Among them was one of the stars of the show, Houston Rockets basketball player Yao Ming. He was an NBA star from China and was back in his home country for this historic event. He was 7-foot-6, so he was hard to miss. He was the flag bearer for the Chinese Olympic Team.

We had to sit in the stands for several hours in the gymnastics venue until it was time for the athletes from each country to file into the stadium and be introduced to the world.

It was really hot in that arena. We were wearing Ralph Lauren blue blazers along with long-sleeved white dress shirts and white pants. We also had on white caps.

All of the athletes looked good, but in my opinion, the Americans were the best-dressed team.

We were sweating like crazy the whole night, especially our heavyweight, Dremiel Byers. It was really warm in there, but we were obviously glad to be there.

We looked sharp, but our outfits weren't designed for the oppressive summer heat.

It was definitely a long night, but we were at the Olympic Games. There definitely were worse places where we could've been that night.

Track and field athlete Lopez Lomong had been selected as the flag bearer for the U.S. team. Lomong, a distance runner, had an incredible story. He escaped from war-torn Sudan, where he nearly died in captivity, and had become a U.S. citizen in 2007.

Overcoming Obstacles to Excel

I posed for a photo with Los Angeles Lakers star Kobe Bryant. NBA star LeBron James was also there.

It was pretty sweet to be there and it was an amazing experience, but I wasn't star-struck or overwhelmed by seeing star athletes from another sport.

It was definitely cool to meet some of those guys and chat with them.

Finally, toward the end of the Opening Ceremonies, the athletes from each country were instructed that they needed to start walking over to the stadium.

The USA contingent was informed it was time to leave the gymnastics venue. We then walked along a red carpet for a short distance to the Olympic Stadium.

Chinese fans spotted Kobe Bryant and started a chant of "Kobe, Kobe!" The NBA had gone global and China was on board, especially with Yao Ming now playing pro ball in the U.S.

Kobe pumped his fist and smiled as fans chanted his name.

The Olympic Stadium was nicknamed the Bird's Nest because of its design. The stadium was filled to capacity with a sellout crowd of 100,000 fans.

When the U.S. team walked into the stadium, I looked up and saw President Bush sitting in the stands. I saw him and I waved at him. I was the only one who waved and he waved back.

So that was unexpected. And really cool.

When we stepped inside the stadium, it was an amazing feeling. I had goosebumps. It was an honor to represent the United States of America at a monumental global sporting event like the Olympic Games.

I had never seen so many people in my life.

We were told this was by far the toughest ticket for fans to obtain for any event of the 2008 Olympics even though it was in the largest venue.

This was a night for China to shine with the entire world watching on television, including the American fans checking out the broadcast on NBC.

The Olympic Games was the biggest sporting event on the plan-

BELIEVE AND ACHIEVE

et and it was being televised live all around the world.

When the U.S. Olympic Team entered the Olympic Stadium, the crowd erupted in cheers. I was walking right next to NBA players Kobe Bryant and Carmelo Anthony as we walked inside.

The host country, China, came in last. The biggest ovation of the night came when Yao Ming entered first, carrying the Chinese flag.

I just enjoyed the moment and tried to take everything in. It was such an honor and a privilege to be a part of that incredible night.

After we were inside the stadium, I remember looking over and seeing actor Jackie Chan performing. He was singing in Chinese. I had only known him from his action movies.

It was very late when the Opening Ceremonies ended. We didn't arrive back at the Olympic Village until well after midnight, but it was still a memorable experience. I was grateful and appreciative to be a part of it.

I couldn't wait to compete in the Olympic Games and that day was going to arrive soon.

The day after the Opening Ceremonies was another day I had been looking forward to.

My family arrived in Beijing.

We had our normal practice schedule that day with workouts in the morning and afternoon.

After the second practice, I took a taxi to the XIJIAO Hotel where my family and friends were staying.

I ate in the city that night for the first time since I had arrived in Beijing.

We had an opportunity to sample several different dishes at an authentic Chinese restaurant. The food was excellent.

The weirdest dish I tried was Donkey, and it was very good. It was similar to a skirt steak with thin slices of beef.

I later sampled a bite of fried scorpion on a stick, but I waited until the day after I wrestled to do that.

It was awesome to see everyone that night at the Chinese restaurant and enjoy a nice meal before I began my final weight-cutting phase. I appreciated my family and friends coming to China to support me. It meant a great deal to have them there.

Overcoming Obstacles to Excel

I hadn't seen my wife in nearly two weeks and it was awesome to spend some time with Marley. It gave me an additional boost in the final days before I would compete.

Now it was time for me to buckle down and begin the drop to 211.5 pounds.

I had a little less than a week to drop close to 20 pounds, but I had a plan in place where I could do it efficiently and effectively.

The final days of my weight cut went really well as I shed the final few pounds before competition.

I did cardio workouts and spent time in the sauna while also reducing my calorie intake.

Everything went smoothly.

I woke up the morning of weigh-ins feeling good. It was the easiest weight cut I ever had because I was so on track and so disciplined with my diet.

We headed over to the wrestling venue for our official weigh-in for the Olympic Games.

It was time to step on the scale.

I was one of 20 Olympians at 96 kilograms/211.5 pounds who stood in line.

Reality was setting in. I was about to wrestle in the Olympics.

We weighed in on the afternoon before our competition.

After each guy weighed in, they grabbed a card off a table that had a number on it. They would hold up the card and show the number to the coaches and the pairings officials who were putting the brackets together.

There was no seeding and the brackets were done by a random draw.

Under that format, athletes could draw the best guy in the bracket. Or the worst guy.

I stepped on the scale and made weight. I grabbed my card and showed the number to everyone.

I was officially in the 96-kilogram bracket for the Olympic Games.

After the draws were done, we knew right away how the brackets looked.

BELIEVE AND ACHIEVE

I had drawn the Hungarian in the first round.

I knew I had a tough match right away. In reality, there were no easy matches at the Olympics. Every country had to qualify for this competition. And every guy was good.

I had drawn Lajos Virag of Hungary, a 2005 World silver medalist, and I knew I would have my hands full.

Virag had defeated Justin Ruiz at the 2005 World Championships.

I had seen Virag wrestle before. He was fundamentally sound. He wasn't super athletic and he wasn't going to launch me with a spectacular throw. But he was a tough, hard-nosed competitor. I knew I was in for a rugged battle.

Virag had gone back-and-forth with Balasz Kiss, his countryman who I had beaten earlier that year at the World Cup.

After I made weight and we saw the brackets, I did what I always did. Hydrate and eat.

I went back to the Olympic Village to eat because I knew it had clean, healthy food. I ate a heavy carbohydrate meal that consisted of pasta and rice.

I believed my body would process the carbs faster for energy. And it would refuel my muscles. It was a better energy source after a prolonged time of a calorie-restricted diet.

I usually would drink water and a supplement similar to Gatorade to rehydrate.

After dinner and after refueling my body, I met up with my family and friends.

I was able to see my wife and my mom briefly. I gave both of them a hug and we said our goodbyes.

After I kissed Marley, she looked in my eyes and said, "Good luck tomorrow. I love you."

"I love you, too," I responded.

I was able to spend about an hour with my family and friends before I went back to my room at the Olympic Village.

All of the work and the prep work was done. I knew who I was wrestling and I knew I had to be ready to go.

There was a lot on my mind, but I was able to shut my brain off enough to fall asleep that night.

I slept really well the night before I competed. Thankfully, I was able to get a good night's sleep.

I was rested and ready.

I woke up the next morning and the moment I had been working for had finally arrived.

It was game day.

I tried to follow a similar routine to what I had done for much of my career.

I tried not to get too amped up or overexcited.

I woke up and did my normal routine.

I ate oatmeal and a banana for breakfast. I brought power bars with me to the venue to snack on for energy during that first session.

I had a clear mind. I was focused on the task at hand.

I went to the venue and did the same warmup I normally did. I warmed up on the practice mats with my training partner, R.C. Johnson.

We stretched and jogged, and then we did some pummeling on our feet and then some par terre work down on the mat. I got my body moving, and my arms and legs warmed up while elevating my heart rate to prepare for my first match.

It was a similar routine that I had used two months before at the Olympic Trials.

I tried to stay as calm and relaxed as possible. Becoming too nervous can eat an athlete alive. It can be physically and mentally draining before a match.

I always had some level of nerves before I wrestled, but for some reason I wasn't nervous for the Olympics.

Maybe it was because I was an underdog and I had nothing to lose.

Win or lose, this was going to be the last tournament of my wrestling career.

I had put 100 percent preparation into my training and I had done everything I could to be ready to compete.

My coaches also had done an amazing job of making sure I was ready. I believed in their plan and they believed in me.

BELIEVE AND ACHIEVE

I remember walking into the arena for my first match with my coach, Momir Petkovic, walking behind me and rubbing my shoulders.

Ivan Ivanov, my coach at Northern Michigan, also was walking into the arena with me.

I felt very confident with those two coaches in the corner. They were two of the top Greco-Roman coaches in the world. They had both wrestled in the Olympics with Momir winning a gold medal in 1976.

They had been on this stage before.

My name was announced over the loudspeakers as I prepared to the step on the mat:

"From the United States of America, Adam Wheeler."

The venue was packed with a sellout crowd of 5,000 enthusiastic fans. I had a small section of family and friends who stood and cheered as I came out to wrestle.

It was an electric atmosphere and the arena was decked out with Olympic logos and colors. There were three full-sized mats where the matches would be held.

I had goosebumps on my arms when I walked into that arena.

I experienced a different feeling than I ever had. It was the greatest feeling of my life. I was about to wrestle in the Olympics and it was an amazing feeling.

I have no idea why, but I wasn't nervous. I was excited, but calm and relaxed. The nerves that I expected weren't there. And that was a very good thing.

The coaches gave me some final words of encouragement.

Momir patted me on the back and leaned toward me.

"Stick to your game plan, Adam," he said, "and you will be successful."

Ivan then added his final words.

"You can do this, Adam," he said. "You've trained for this moment."

They were right. I was ready to go.

I nodded my head at my coaches before I turned toward the mat. I ran up the stairs, walked onto the elevated mat and shook the referee's hand.

It was time.

I shook hands with my opponent and the whistle blew to start the match.

I immediately went on the attack on my feet. I was aggressive and looking to score. Virag was wrestling defensively and trying to take the match to the par terre portion of the period.

I was pummeling under his arms when we were on our feet. I was trying to put pressure on him to eventually wear him out.

It was one of those matches where I was lucky. Two of the three ball draws came out in my favor.

We split the first two periods, where the score ended 1-1 both times with each of us winning on criteria.

The match came down to the third period and I won the ball draw. The referee pulled a blue ball out of the bag that matched my singlet color.

I was down in par terre last and he was unable to turn me.

I knew I had to defend him to win the match or my Olympic gold-medal chances were done. I was able to stop his gut-wrench and I stopped him from scoring.

Time ran out.

I had knocked off a World silver medalist in my Olympic debut.

It was a huge win for me and I pumped my right fist, but that was it. I didn't celebrate. I still had a long way to go in that tournament.

That win confirmed what I already believed. That I was ready to win a gold medal.

I had to immediately shift my focus to the next match. Next up was a quarterfinal match with China's Jiang Huachen.

I hadn't really paid much attention to the brackets before the tournament. All of my focus was on a tough first-round opponent from Hungary.

I figured if I beat him, then I would worry about my next opponent.

The wrestler from China was a big, physical guy. I had actually trained with him in Colorado Springs at the Olympic Training Center.

I had practiced with him and I had the upper-hand on him in the wrestling room, but he was still a dangerous wrestler with some good moves.

It wasn't unusual to see a foreign wrestler who wasn't very good in the practice room perform much better in competition.

Jiang was one of those guys.

He came out and won the first period decisively by a 7-0 score.

Not only did I lose the period, I was in serious pain.

I had torn cartilage in my ribs during training before the Olympics and Jiang had launched me with a vicious reverse lift in the opening period.

He jumped out in front of me and when he was lifting me, I felt my ribs pop. He kicked my butt, but it wasn't the first time I had lost the first period.

I knew I could come back. I rallied to beat Robby Smith at the Olympic Trials after he won the first period against me.

When I walked back to my corner after the first period, Momir and Ivan had me make an adjustment.

"You need to push back when he does that."

They were right. I knew he caught me and made a great move, but it couldn't happen again or I was done.

In the second period, he tried to throw me again and I followed my coaches' advice. I was able to push back and counter him. I ended up on top of him in a scramble.

That was a match where I definitely had to stay tough and mentally keep my focus. He beat me handily in the first period, but I had to make sure I didn't break mentally.

I came back to win the second period 3-2 to even the match at one period apiece.

It all came down to the third period.

Neither one of us could score during the first minute on our feet, but I was staying aggressive and active to tire him out.

I was so confident that I couldn't get tired. My conditioning was on point and I felt great. I was setting a frenetic pace to try and break him.

Now it came down to another ball draw.

The referee reached his right hand into a small bag and then pulled a ball out that was red to match the color of my singlet.

I had the advantage, but I still had to execute.

I was on top in the first 30 seconds and I was looking for a turn, but he was able to defend me.

Now it came down to the last 30 seconds. I had to stop him from turning me.

I held my ground and I was able to stop him.

The horn sounded as time ran out.

I won the match by virtue of scoring last.

I had advanced to the Olympic semifinals.

That was another huge win for me. I was one win from the finals and two wins from capturing a gold medal.

My ribs were killing me after that second match. They gave me a shot in my ribs that was supposed to numb the pain. But it didn't help me.

I had to grit my teeth and fight through it. I had worked too hard to give up on my dreams.

My semifinal match would be against Mirko Englich of Germany. He was a 2004 Olympian who had placed fifth at the 2005 World Championships.

I knew Mirko was a good wrestler who was experienced, but I was confident that I could beat him.

I had never wrestled Mirko in a competition, but I was familiar with him.

The German team had come to the U.S. Olympic Training Center and I had wrestled against him in practice.

I knew he was a tough wrestler because he had beaten Justin Ruiz. That immediately gained my attention because Justin had been a World bronze medalist and went on to place fifth in the World later in his career.

I walked onto the mat for my third match of the session and I was ready to roll.

I had already beaten two tough guys and my confidence level was high.

I was one win away from advancing to the gold medal match at the Olympic Games.

The match against Mirko was going to be another strategic battle.

BELIEVE AND ACHIEVE

We finished the first minute of the match with nobody scoring, so we went to yet another ball draw.

The referee pulled out a blue ball and I had won the draw. I was wearing the blue singlet.

I would be in the top position for the first 30 seconds and I was determined to turn him.

I locked my arms around his chest and tried valiantly to turn Mirko to his back to gain exposure points.

As I tried to turn him, he countered my attempt and I lost control. He was able to reverse me for a point.

I was down in the last 30 seconds and he wasn't able to turn me, but he had scored two points when I was on top. That gave him a 2-1 win in the first period.

We walked back to our corners between periods and I was frustrated. I felt like I gave that period away by being too aggressive. I had won the ball draw. All I had to do was not get turned and I would've won the period.

Believe it or not, the second period played out in similar fashion.

After another scoreless opening minute on our feet, the referee once again pulled a blue ball out of the bag.

I had the advantage again.

I was on top first and went for the same turn that I did in the first period. And he reversed me again to take a 2-0 lead en route to winning the period.

Englich won the match 2-1, 2-1 by capitalizing on my mistakes.

I felt horrible.

I had wasted a golden opportunity.

I had a high gut-wrench on him and I was determined that I could pull him backwards. I was confident that I could score against Mirko.

I really believed I was going to score with that move.

I believed in it so much that I tried it twice and it backfired both times.

In hindsight, maybe I shouldn't have tried scoring like that.

But at the time, it felt right and I felt like I could score.

I just hate that I made a mistake like that.

I'm not taking anything from Mirko. He was a great wrestler and he was very experienced.

He deserved to win an Olympic medal and he did an amazing job.

As the match ended, I stood with my hands on my hips as Mirko raised both arms in celebration.

Mirko Englich was headed to the gold-medal match.

And I would be wrestling for bronze.

My dreams of winning a gold medal at the Olympics were dashed.

It was a crushing loss. All of my training was geared toward winning an Olympic gold medal.

But now I had to reset my goals.

I didn't want to leave Beijing empty-handed and I still had a chance to fly home with an Olympic medal hanging around my neck.

Losing that match really sucked, especially when I felt like I could have won.

I was fighting back tears as we walked off the mat.

I was on such a huge high before I lost.

I ran into the Hungarian back in the warmup area.

"I'm sorry," I told him.

He needed me to make the finals for him to have a chance to wrestle back.

But I couldn't spend a lot of time feeling sorry for myself or anyone else. I had to regroup for my bronze medal match. I felt like I had been overconfident going into that match against Mirko. He wrestled smart and was able to beat me. On paper, that was my easiest match. I was really upset when I lost.

The good news was that I had a few hours to regroup between sessions. I went back to our team leader John Bardis' hotel room and I was able to eat and then take a shower. I also had time to take a nap before the medal matches. It had been a long day already and I was worn down physically and mentally after three tough matches.

I had reinjured my ribs in the quarterfinals and then suffered a devastating loss in the semifinals.

Our coaches were trying to pump me up and encourage me. They were talking to me about staying professional. I still had a job to do for my team and my country. There was one more match to wrestle and there was a medal out there waiting to be won.

The U.S. Greco Team had been shut out in the medal department at the Olympics and I was our last hope.

I had worked too hard and been through too much to give up now.

I was able to rest and regroup. And regain my composure.

And my coaches were there to help me bounce back from a tough loss.

My coach, Ivan Ivanov, also delivered a message to me during the break.

His words really resonated with me.

"Trust me," Ivan told me, "you don't want to get fifth."

I knew exactly what he meant and I took it to heart.

I knew Ivan placed fifth at the Olympics when he had competed for Bulgaria. I knew that still haunted him.

He had fallen just short of winning a medal.

There would be two bronze medal matches in each weight class in Beijing and the loser of each match would finish fifth.

I definitely didn't want to be one of those guys who took fifth.

My bronze-medal bout would be against Han Tae-Young of Korea.

The U.S. coaches knew the Korean well because he had defeated Justin Ruiz in three periods in a second-round match at the 2006 World Championships in Guangzhou, China.

Young had defended against Justin after winning a coin flip in the third period. Justin had turned him early in the match, but the Korean had won back-to-back coin flips en route to winning the last two periods.

That was Young's game – winning with his defense.

The Korean's luck continued when I met him with an Olympic medal on the line.

In the first period, Young won the ball draw after a scoreless first minute on our feet.

By winning the ball draw, the Korean would be down in the last 30 seconds. He looked over in his corner, smiled and clapped his hands because he was confident that he couldn't be turned.

That's how he had beaten Ruiz in 2006.

The Korean believed he was going to win that period.

I had my own game plan and I knew what I was going to do. I was going to do a reverse headlock and pull him back. It was not a move you saw a lot and it was one he wouldn't be ready to defend.

When I hit that move, it surprised him. I was able to turn him and score.

I won the first period.

During the first period, Young actually bit me. I was trying to get my lock to turn him, and he bit my finger. I didn't hurt that much, probably because I had so much adrenaline. But it definitely annoyed me. It was enough to make me think, "What the hell is this guy doing? And why didn't the ref see it?"

It was just another obstacle for me to overcome. I couldn't worry about it.

The second period was scoreless after a minute and the ball draw came up blue. That was my color.

This time, I had won the ball draw.

I didn't clap or smile, like my opponent had the period before, but I did like my chances.

The Korean was in the down position first and I was unable to turn him. I started with a reverse lock, but he was very difficult to move.

Now I just had to defend and keep him from scoring in the final 30 seconds. If I did, I would win the match and win a bronze medal.

The whistle blew and Young jumped in front of me and aggressively tried to reverse lift me. My heart was pounding and sweat was pouring off me as I fought valiantly to hold my position.

I was in the best shape of my life and nobody was going to break me.

Not only was I able to stop Young from turning me, but I countered his move and put him on his back for a couple of seconds. I knew at that point I was going to win the match.

Young fought back to his belly and then I went behind him. Time was running out. I wrapped my arms around him in a gut-wrench position as the final seconds ticked off the clock.

I looked up at the scoreboard and the horn sounded.

Time had run out.

I won the match 4-1, 3-1.

I jumped to my feet and raised both arms above my head before running over to my corner to give Momir and Ivan a hug.

I wrapped my arms around both coaches simultaneously. I would've never made it to this point without Momir and Ivan.

"Great job, Adam!" both coaches told me as we hugged. "Great job!"

I smiled and pumped my right fist toward my section of fans as I ran back to the center of the mat to have my hand raised in victory.

I had a small, but enthusiastic group of 19 family and friends who had come to Beijing to watch me wrestle. And I could see all of them standing and cheering for me.

I had won an Olympic bronze medal.

It was an exciting and amazing moment. I was pumped. It was even better than I imagined.

It was a moment I had envisioned. And a moment I had dreamed of.

I didn't reach my goal of winning an Olympic gold medal.

But I had won a bronze medal at the Olympic Games.

It was one of the best feelings I've ever had in my lifetime.

I had an avalanche of emotions running through me.

I was overwhelmed with joy and satisfaction.

It was an incredible feeling.

And I was walking off a wrestling mat for the final time as a competitive athlete.

I had wrestled my final match.

I had come a long way from being an overweight high school freshman who couldn't run one lap around a track or do a pushup.

And from being a guy one of my high school coaches didn't think was good enough to go to a summer wrestling camp.

I had more than my share of doubters and detractors along the way to a spot on the medal podium at the Olympic Games.

Greco-Roman was the first style to take the mat at the 2008

Olympics, so I became the first wrestling medalist for the United States in 2008.

I was overwhelmed with excitement.

All of the hard work and sacrifice had paid off for me.

I had a huge smile on my face and I looked up in the stands again while waving to my wife, my mom, and my family and friends.

Someone handed me an American flag and I wrapped it around me.

I was just so happy when I won that medal.

It was an amazing moment.

Right after the match, 2000 Olympic gold medalist Rulon Gardner interviewed me on NBC. It was awesome that he was the one asking me questions.

Rulon had become a mentor to me. I had developed a good relationship with him and we had talked on the phone numerous times that year. He offered me a lot of advice that helped me when I competed at the Olympics.

After the interview, one of our coaches, Brandon Paulson, called out to me from the stands. Brandon was an awesome guy who I really looked up to. He won an Olympic silver medal during his career.

"You did it, Adam!" Brandon said enthusiastically.

"You did it!"

That felt good to hear from someone like Brandon who I had great respect for.

He knew first-hand how difficult it was to win a medal at the Olympic Games.

I was super pumped to win an Olympic bronze medal. I thought about where I had come from and all that I overcame.

I had so many sources of motivation that fueled me during my Olympic quest.

Standing on the podium during the medal ceremony, my head was spinning as I tried to process everything that had just happened.

It had been quite a journey.

Russia's Aslanbek Khushtov defeated Germany's Mirko Englich to win the gold medal at my weight class of 96 kilograms, so the Russian national anthem was played after we received our medals.

BELIEVE AND ACHIEVE

During the anthem, the red, white and blue American flag was raised alongside the flags of the gold medalist from Russia, the silver medalist from Germany and the other bronze medalist from Kazakhstan.

A bronze medal was placed around my neck and I was handed a beautiful glass vase holding six red roses.

I tried to soak up the experience of being on the podium and enjoy the moment.

Even though I received a bronze medal, and it was third place, I still had such a sense of accomplishment.

Nobody trains to win a bronze medal, but it was a nice reward for me after I rebounded from a stinging loss in the semifinals.

I was happy with my overall performance and I left everything I had out on the mat.

I know some wrestlers say it haunts them if they don't win the gold medal.

But I knew I had accomplished something pretty special to be on the Olympic podium.

The feeling was even better than I had imagined it would be.

During the anthem, I wished it was our national anthem. But I wasn't sad.

It was an honor to be on that medal podium with some of the best wrestlers on the planet.

We were taken to a press conference in the wrestling venue after the medal ceremony.

During the press conference, my wife and my mom walked in the back of the room. Tears started coming down my face and that's when the emotion started setting in. Marley and my mom were a huge part of this journey. This was a victory for all of us.

Nobody had asked me a question during the press conference before the Olympics.

But like I had told Coach Fraser that day, the media would want to talk to me at the press conference after I wrestled.

And they did.

When the media asked me how I felt, I had a simple reply.

"I'm on top of the world," I told the media. "This is an amazing feeling to win a medal for my country."

I talked about the support I had received during the press conference.

"My wife and my mother are here," I said. "We have 19 people who came here for me, and it can't get any better than that."

My coaches also met with the media.

"I am very happy for Adam," Coach Fraser said. "He has worked hard for many years, especially the last few months. He has a great attitude. He is a wonderful, coachable kid."

Ivan Ivanov was asked about the road I had followed on my way to becoming an Olympic medalist.

"Not many people believed in Adam," Ivan said. "He believed in himself. He believed he was going to beat this guy. He believed he was going to bring that medal back."

When Marley and I finally came face-to-face, we shared a long embrace as we both had tears in our eyes.

I gave her a kiss.

"I love you, Marley," I said.

"I love you, too," she said.

And then I gave my mom a hug. She had been there with me for so many years and had always been my No. 1 fan.

"I love you, Mom," I said. "Thank you!"

"I'm so proud of you!" she responded.

After the press conference, I was taken into a room at the venue by an official from the World Anti-Doping Agency for drug testing. Fortunately for me, it didn't take me very long.

All of the Olympic medalists were tested for performance-enhancing drugs.

I then did a short media tour at the Main Press Center where I did a number of television interviews.

My wife, my mom and R.C. Johnson were all with us, along with Communications Manager Craig Sesker of USA Wrestling.

We were in the green room waiting to do an interview with NBC and they showed a replay of my bronze medal match on the television.

It was fun to watch the match while reliving that moment just a short time after I had wrestled.

BELIEVE AND ACHIEVE

It was awesome seeing myself on TV wrestling in the Olympics.

After I won the bronze medal, it was still early in the morning in the U.S. The time in China was 13 hours ahead of where I lived in Colorado.

People didn't have Twitter or Instagram back then, so most of my family and friends were clicking on USA Wrestling's website to find out how I had fared.

Information wasn't as easily accessible as it is now.

I had a cellular phone, but it wasn't exactly state of the art. I had a little flip phone.

When we were at the Main Press Center, there was a table in the green room filled with an assortment of snacks and treats.

R.C. got his money's worth, chowing down on candy bars and ice cream bars. We were joking that he set an unofficial Olympic record for most calories consumed in a green room.

R.C. had earned it. He was an awesome training partner for me and he played a huge role in helping me prepare for the Olympic Games. I can't thank him enough for being so selfless.

I should have saved all of those Snickers bars I had at the Olympic Village for him.

After we were done with the media obligations, we jumped in a van and were driven to USA House for a celebration dinner.

It was very late and our entire Greco-Roman team was there along with USA Wrestling staff members and members of the U.S. Olympic Committee.

It had been a very long day, but it was more than worth it. It was the last day for the Greco competition, so it also served as our social for the team.

I was up very late that night.

I missed out on some time with my family and friends the night I competed because of my media obligations, but I was able to see many of them after I arrived at USA House.

I posed for photos with Willie Madison and Mark Rial, two good friends of mine who were training partners for the U.S. team.

I was so grateful for all of the people who came to watch me wrestle in Beijing.

Overcoming Obstacles to Excel

That group included my wife, Marley, and my mom, Julie, along with John Bailey, Diana Bailey, Donald Bailey, Garry Peterson, Amy Peterson, Mike Henery Sr, Jane Henery, Mike Henery Jr., Michelle Henery, Alexa Henery, Chloe Henery, Matt Henery, Tara Henery, Jameson Henery, Jim Clifford, Carol Raanes, Mamie Garceo and Donna Pope.

It was awesome to have them there when I competed in the biggest tournament of my life.

When I was talking to my family and friends at USA House, they told me a pretty cool story about what happened during the medal matches at 96 kilograms.

My family and friends had good seats for the Olympics. After my bronze medal match, my family and friends asked Mirko Englich's family if they wanted to sit in those seats to watch Mirko's gold medal match.

Mirko's family had seats farther away from the mat.

It was a really nice gesture. And I know they appreciated it.

I stayed just a short time in Beijing after I was done wrestling.

It was an amazing experience, but I was ready to go home.

I was in China for 18 days.

There was one more memorable moment for me before we departed China and headed back to the United States.

After we boarded the plane for our flight from Beijing to San Francisco, one of my teammates came up to talk to me.

It was our heavyweight, Dremiel Byers.

Dremiel had an outstanding career for the U.S. and would've done even better if he wouldn't have had to battle Olympic and World champion Rulon Gardner for all of those years.

Dremiel won a World title in 2002 and he won a World bronze medal in 2007 to help the U.S. win the team title at the World Championships.

I really looked up to him and he made me a better wrestler every time I trained with him. He was a big dude with a big presence and a larger-than-life personality.

Dremiel was a loud, boisterous guy with a great sense of humor. He also was a talented wrestler who delivered by winning his share of

BELIEVE AND ACHIEVE

big matches for Team USA.

When I first started wrestling Greco-Roman on the Senior circuit, Dremiel already was an established star in the sport.

He was on the cover of USA Wrestling's magazine after he won Worlds in 2002. I hung that magazine cover up on the wall in my room when I was wrestling for the Navy team.

I used to see Dremiel a lot in those early days because he wrestled for the U.S. Army team as part of the World Class Athlete Program.

We would both compete in the Armed Forces Championships.

When we were boarding the plane to leave Beijing after the 2008 Olympics, Dremiel walked up and gave me a hug.

"You did it, man!" he said. "Good job!"

"Thank you!" I responded.

That was really cool because one of the guys that I had really looked up to and admired in wrestling had congratulated me.

It was a selfless gesture by Dremiel, who won his first two matches at the Olympics before coming up just short of winning a medal in Beijing.

Being the great champion that he was, Dremiel stormed back the following year to win a silver medal at the 2009 World Championships before making his second straight Olympic Team in 2012. He had a Hall of Fame career.

It meant a lot to me when Dremiel congratulated me at the Olympics.

That was the perfect way to cap off an unbelievable and unforgettable experience.

CHAPTER 6
After Beijing

It was great to be home and be back on U.S. soil, but I didn't have much of a break. Shortly after returning home, I was on the move again.

I had been hired by the Colorado Springs Police Department on June 12, 2008. That was three days before I competed at the Olympic Trials.

I was scheduled to report to the Police Academy just a short time after the Olympic Games, so everything worked out.

I had just enough time to wrestle in the two biggest competitions of my life.

I didn't receive any special exceptions with the police department because I was on the Olympic Team.

While I was preparing to compete in the Olympic Games, I did think about my upcoming career in law enforcement.

My family was heavily involved in public service. I had family in the military and also had relatives who were police officers and fire-fighters.

I was looking forward to starting my career as a police officer.

I was going to start making a full-time income. I was ready.

I had actually considered becoming a cop in 2003 when I was leaving the military, but thankfully I decided to continue wrestling.

It all worked out in the end.

Luckily, my wife was working full-time as a teacher during my days as an Olympic-level athlete.

BELIEVE AND ACHIEVE

It was tough on us financially with me not having a full-time income.

I probably needed a new car, but I just couldn't afford it. I was driving a 1991 Toyota Corolla with a ton of miles on it. But the car was still running and it was getting me to where I needed to be.

Back in those days, athletes didn't make a whole lot of money wrestling full-time.

That was definitely the case for me.

Until I made the Olympic Team.

Before Beijing, I received a monthly stipend of $1,000 from USA Wrestling for being the No. 2 guy at my weight class.

And I worked as a part-time personal trainer at 24-Hour Fitness. When I first started working there, I did a lot of training sessions.

I would make $25 an hour to train a client, but I was forced to cut back on the number of training sessions I did because I had to devote more time to my training.

Early in 2008, 24-Hour Fitness became one of my sponsors. They paid me $1,000 a month to sponsor me as an athlete. That provided a huge boost for me and it eased my financial burden. I also continued to earn money from 24-Hour Fitness as a trainer.

I made most of my money in wrestling from the Olympic bronze medal that I won.

I received some fairly lucrative bonuses in 2008 – for making the Olympic Team and after I won a medal.

It was awesome to be able to cash in after struggling to earn much money in previous years.

With the bonus money I received after winning the bronze medal, Marley and I were able to pay off some of our debt.

I received bonuses from 24-Hour Fitness after the Olympics that totaled $25,000. That was super generous and gracious of them.

Gator Wrestling Club gave me a bonus of $10,000. That provided a nice boost as well. Jim Ravannack, who ran the Gator club, took good care of me when I wrestled for them. Jim also paid for me to go to Baku as a training partner for the 2007 World Championships. I'm incredibly grateful to Jim. That trip helped pave the way for my Olympic run the following year.

Overcoming Obstacles to Excel

I also received a $10,000 bonus check from the U.S. Olympic Committee for medaling. And USA Wrestling gave me a bonus check of $6,000.

It was awesome to be rewarded for my performance at the Olympics. I obviously wasn't competing for the money, but the compensation I received after Beijing was a nice reward for what I accomplished.

Bouncing back from that tough semifinal loss to prevail in the bronze-medal match really paid off for me and my family.

I received one final, and unexpected, surprise after the Olympics.

Our awesome team leader, John Bardis, presented me with an amazing gift a short time after I won my medal. John gave me an expensive watch after the Olympics. It was a Panerai luxury watch. I Googled it and the retail price for that watch was $9,000. It was an incredible gesture by John. The watch came in a beautiful wooden box with a silver plaque on top.

There was engraving on it that read:

Adam Wheeler
Bronze Medalist 96 kg
Greco-Roman Wrestling
2008 Olympics.

I had no idea John was sending me that watch. It was so thoughtful of him to do that. I was blown away.

It's a beautiful watch.

I was actually afraid to wear the watch at first because it was so expensive.

John Bardis was the best team leader ever. He's a great man who I am still friends with. He's one of the best people I've ever been around.

John has made so many positive contributions to wrestling. I'm very grateful that he was with us on our Olympic journey in Beijing.

I wrestled at the Olympic Games on August 14, 2008, and I returned home two days later.

We went back in time on the way home with the radical time change, but I was so tired when we landed in the U.S. that I didn't really notice.

BELIEVE AND ACHIEVE

We had another long flight from Beijing to San Francisco. We went through customs in California and then completed the trip with a much shorter flight from San Francisco to Colorado Springs.

It was so good to be home.

I love traveling to other countries, but it is always great to be back in the USA.

I had a short time at home in Colorado Springs before I started my training at the Police Academy on August 27.

I had retired from wrestling, but there were a number of people in the sport who thought maybe I was stepping away too soon.

I had just started hitting my peak at age 27.

A short time after we returned home, Momir Petkovic talked with me. And, as Mo always did, he gave it to me straight.

"You're just getting to the point in your career where you're really good," Momir told me matter-of-factly, "and now you're leaving."

I had a tremendous level of respect for Momir and what he said made perfect sense to me. I could have continued to wrestle and continued to compete at a high level with Momir coaching me.

But I was ready for the next phase of my life.

I also had people talk to me about going into mixed martial arts. Competing in the Ultimate Fighting Championships was something that appealed to me. I enjoyed watching it and a number of wrestlers had enjoyed great success in the UFC, including Randy Couture. Randy was a top Greco-Roman wrestler on the Senior level before winning a UFC title.

Two freestyle wrestlers from the 2008 Olympic Team—World bronze medalist Daniel Cormier and Olympic gold medalist Henry Cejudo – went on to win championships in the UFC.

MMA was definitely something that I was interested in and had thought about.

About a year and a half after the Olympics, freestyle wrestler Nick Simmons put me in contact with the people from World Wrestling Entertainment. The WWE was a big-time professional wrestling league that received tons of exposure on television and was a multimillion-dollar company.

Hulk Hogan, John Cena and Dwayne "The Rock" Johnson were

among the superstars who wrestled in the WWE, a league that differed from the style of wrestling I had competed in.

Kurt Angle, a 1996 Olympic gold medalist in freestyle wrestling, was a WWE champion.

WWE matches were contested in a square "ring" similar to what they use in boxing with ropes on each of the four sides. It was more of a show than a competition, but their superstars were famous and made a great living.

The WWE offered me a deal for $750 a week, but there was no insurance. I would've had to move to Florida where their training facility was located.

I talked to Bobby Lashley, an Olympic-style wrestler I knew who had gone on to a successful career in the WWE. Bobby was doing well, but he also told me about some of his experiences. He said it was a grind and that he was on the road 300 days a year as a pro wrestler. It wasn't as glamorous as it might appear.

One of my teammates at Northern Michigan, Chas Betts, pursued a career in the WWE and has gone on to excel as one of their top attractions. He competes in the WWE under the wrestling name of Chad Gable and has become popular with fans.

Chas was a 2012 Olympian for the U.S. in Greco-Roman wrestling. You can see his wrestling skills on display when he launches his opponents during his WWE matches.

When I talked to the WWE in 2010, I had only been with the police department a short time. Not to mention that my son, Jameson, had just been born. And Marley and I had just purchased a house.

My wife and I talked about it, but I ultimately decided to turn down the offer from the WWE.

Looking back, part of me regrets turning some of that stuff down.

But at the time, Marley and I both already had good jobs with insurance. And we had just started a family.

Some of those ventures that I could have pursued after the Olympics would have been risky for us financially.

Maybe I should have taken the risk, but I turned down those opportunities to have a stable income. I did what was best for my family.

BELIEVE AND ACHIEVE

I had grown up poor and I think that was in the back of my mind. I obviously never wanted to go back to living like that.

I wanted to take care of my family from a financial standpoint.

My focus had shifted from being an athlete to working in law enforcement.

When I joined the Police Academy, I figured the training would have some challenges. And it did.

I thought that the academy would be like a military boot camp and be very regimented.

But I showed up the first day and it was nothing like that.

I walked in the door and the sergeant told me that the academy used to be more physically demanding.

We still did some fitness work, but it wasn't overly taxing. We did two weeks of shooting. We learned arrest control techniques.

Driving was the most enjoyable part of the academy. It was blast. We learned first-hand how fast those police cars go and what we could do with them.

I didn't expect them to go that fast. We were weaving in and out of cones, and it was exciting.

The speed you can maneuver those cars at is impressive.

We drove the old Ford Crown Victoria model with V8 engines. They had some serious power.

We typically went to the academy Monday through Friday from 8 a.m. to 4 p.m.

About 70 percent of the time at the academy was spent in the classroom. Some of the material was very interesting. And some of it wasn't.

I already had my bachelor's degree in criminal justice, so I knew some of the material. Not a lot of it, but enough where I had a decent grasp of it.

When I was at the academy, I met people who became some of my best friends.

I was transitioning from being an athlete to being a police officer and I instantly clicked with a few of the guys that I still hang out with.

It was a fun time. I was eager to start my career as a police officer.

Physically, it wasn't terribly challenging. We had to do a fitness test. It was easy because I was already in great shape after just finishing with the Olympics.

I had to be able to do a certain number of pushups, sit-ups and pull-ups to score 100 percent.

I had to do a 300-meter sprint. And a mile and a half run.

We had to do the test three times.

I was able to score 100 percent on the test every time.

They were trying to measure our progress and improvement in terms of fitness.

A lot of people improved because they weren't in very good shape when they started.

I actually did extra workouts, like lifting weights on my lunch break, when I was at the Police Academy.

We learned how to shoot with a nine-millimeter handgun. I had already learned how to shoot at boot camp when I was in the Coast Guard, but I hadn't done much shooting during my time in the military.

I wasn't that good when I started in the academy, but I ended up being the second-best shooter in my class of 16.

After the academy, I had four months of additional police training.

I rode along on patrol with one partner for two months and then rode along with another partner for two months.

I was finally ready to go out on my own.

I was assigned to patrol a specific area of Colorado Springs.

I was on the midnight shift my first year as a cop. At first, I thought it was cool. But then it sets in quick that you are out there by yourself.

I had to be on my A game.

I had been in the northeast part of town on patrol by myself for about six months before I worked in the downtown area for a year.

It was a little scary and a little bit nerve-wracking, but I wasn't ever in fear for my life.

After a year downtown, I was asked where I wanted to work and I picked the Sand Creek area. That was the busiest area in terms of crime and incidents involving the police.

I wanted to do police work and feel like I was making a difference.

BELIEVE AND ACHIEVE

I started in Sand Creek in 2011 and I had the most fun that year. A lot of my friends were working out there and it was an enjoyable place to work.

In late 2012, I was on patrol when two serious incidents happened.

The first incident was the first time where I could have died in the line of duty.

I was on a regular night of patrol and it was around midnight.

I heard a call go out on the radio about a car-jacking that occurred earlier in the evening. A man had pointed a gun at someone and stolen his truck.

I then heard another call on the radio that another officer had closed in behind the stolen truck.

A short time later, we were informed that the suspect in the truck had opened fire on the police officer.

The other officer and I sprang into action. We turned on our lights and sirens and rushed to help.

As we were driving, we heard another call that the suspect had taken off in the stolen vehicle and was at a location near us. Shortly after that, I entered an intersection.

The suspect in the truck was coming right at me and nearly hit me.

The truck made a sharp turn and then somehow was positioned right behind me.

The suspect had already been shooting at the police and I thought he might start shooting at me.

I lowered myself down in the seat and looked in my rearview mirror as I accelerated to create distance.

Another police officer heard the suspect fire again, this time toward me. The officer came up and bumped the truck from behind, causing the suspect's vehicle to spin and become disabled.

The officer's vehicle and the suspect's truck had both crashed and had come to a stop. They were sitting right next to each other.

I made a quick U-turn in the middle of the street and I could see how the vehicles ended up. I was fearing the suspect was going to shoot the officer who was sitting just a few feet away from him.

I wasn't going to let that happen.

I floored the accelerator, quickly picked up speed and slammed my car directly into the door of the suspect's truck.

That resulted in a loud collision and chaos ensued.

I had to act quickly because I knew he could potentially kill the other cop.

After I drilled the truck with my car, the air bag in my car deployed. Now I had lost a visual of the suspect. My door was stuck and it wouldn't open at first because I had smashed it when I hit the truck.

Eventually, I was able to force the door open. I saw other police officers had closed in and had surrounded the suspect before arresting him.

I learned later that another cop had witnessed the suspect raising his gun to shoot the other officer just as I slammed my vehicle into his truck.

That prevented the suspect from shooting the police officer and led to him being arrested.

It was a wild, scary and crazy scene and I became really light-headed after that incident.

I was put in a neck brace and placed on a backboard. I was transported to the hospital as a precaution.

Luckily, I didn't sustain any serious injuries. I was a little sore the next day, but that was about it.

After that incident, it really hit home for me just how dangerous my job was.

That was the first time I had really felt that way in my time as a police officer.

And it made me immediately think about my family.

My wife and I had a 3-year-old son and a 1-year-old son at the time. That really put everything in perspective. It made me emotional and made me think about what I was doing.

I was awarded a medal of valor for my role in helping apprehend the suspect in that incident.

There was another serious incident about a month later. It was late at night again. We received a call that shots had been fired in the southeast part of Colorado Springs near the Olympic Training Center.

It turned into another high-speed pursuit and I was coming from another area to provide assistance.

Alan, the same cop involved in the incident a month earlier, did the same maneuver to make the suspect's car crash. He bumped into the guy's car to make him wreck.

The suspect quickly jumped out of his car and took off running. And we ran after him.

I was one of 10 officers in a pursuit on foot.

We were chasing the suspect for a while. We climbed over a wall, went down an alley and ran through a parking lot.

The guy was really moving, and running pretty fast, and not all of the officers could keep pace. Alan and I were the only ones still chasing the suspect after a few minutes.

Another officer eventually pulled up in a car, and the suspect stopped. The officer told the suspect he needed to surrender or he would use a taser to subdue him.

The suspect was asked to surrender several times and he refused the commands while shouting profanities at us.

He then yelled at us, "I'm gonna shoot you!"

We yelled back at the suspect, "Let me see your hands!"

After several more of our commands and several more opportunities for him to surrender, the suspect refused to show us his hands.

He was armed, and he turned back toward me and the other officer. We believed he had a gun in his hand. He again yelled that he was going to shoot us.

At that point, we didn't have a choice. We fired at the suspect and shot him.

He fell to the ground. He was still yelling at us and still reaching for his gun.

Eventually, we were able to close in on him and place the suspect in handcuffs.

Alan and I both received a medal of valor for that incident.

I learned how unpredictable that life in law enforcement can be. I had to be ready for anything at any time.

During my early days as a police officer, I had also gone back to school and earned my master's degree in 2011. I earned a master's in public administration from the University of Colorado at Colorado Springs.

Not bad for a guy who once dropped out of high school.

During that time, I tested for a position with the Federal Bureau of Investigation. I passed my test and was given an interview.

After talking with my wife, I took my name out of the process for the FBI.

I was looking for a way to advance myself in law enforcement, but I would have had to move around a lot if I would have been hired by the FBI.

That would've been extremely tough for a young family.

I set a goal to become a detective when I joined the police department, but that changed after another opportunity presented itself.

I had a chance to work with the SWAT team for two weeks and that was a job that really appealed to me.

I was with them on a temporary duty assignment and I was able to see how they worked.

Landing a spot on the SWAT team is not easy.

A SWAT (Special Weapons and Tactics) team is a law enforcement unit that uses specialized or military equipment and tactics.

The first time I was able to test with the SWAT team was in 2012 and I was the only candidate who maxed out on the entire fitness test.

For the SWAT test, I needed to successfully complete the following challenges to pass:

A vertical jump over 25½ inches.

88 pushups in two minutes.

A back squat 1½ times my body weight. I had to do around 360 pounds.

Six pull-ups while wearing a 40-pound vest.

A front plank (for abdominal muscles) for two minutes.

A side plank on each side for 1 minute, 36 seconds apiece.

A 300-meter sprint in 44 seconds.

A 20-meter shuttle run test where I went down and back while steadily increasing my speed.

The last two requirements on the list were the most difficult.

BELIEVE AND ACHIEVE

I did some specific training for a couple of months to prepare for the SWAT testing.

It was the summer of 2012 and I was still on patrol as a police officer.

The second phase of the SWAT test was the shooting portion of the test.

That was another difficult phase.

We had to move while we were shooting. We also would sprint up and down hills and then do 10 pushups before shooting.

We also had to simulate real-life scenarios.

It was much more challenging than just standing there and shooting at a target that wasn't moving.

I passed the shooting test on my first try. It was right after the fitness test on the same day.

The most important aspect of the test was the oral interview.

I did the interview a few weeks later.

They asked us a lot of tactical questions. I had to know that side of police work to be on the SWAT team.

I was one of the only applicants testing for the first time. It was nerve-wracking and stressful.

I had only been a cop for four years and I was applying for one of the most difficult positions in the police department.

I was nervous because I really wanted that position and I worked hard at being ready for my opportunity.

I studied really hard before the interview. I did some mock interviews and I also had practiced it in my head.

I did everything I could to prepare.

Some of that went back to my days as an athlete.

If you want something, you have to work hard at it. It's not going to be handed to you. Especially a position like that.

The interview lasted 15 minutes and I passed.

There were around a dozen people that tested for the SWAT team and I was one of only a handful that passed.

I felt confident that I did well. I was the only applicant that maxed out on the fitness test.

I had passed the tests, but there was still no guarantee I was going to be hired for the SWAT team.

Normally, there would only be about one opening a year.

I was lucky because they had four openings for the SWAT team that year and I was the third one selected.

That was unheard of, for four people to be hired in a year.

I was informed in October 2012 that I would be joining the SWAT team and I started with them in January 2013.

The timing was perfect for me because I was looking for the next challenge in my career.

Joining the SWAT team gave me new life in the police world and I thought it was something I could do for a long time.

During the time I was in the police academy, I also found other ways to stay active.

I was finished with wrestling after the 2008 Olympic Games, but I needed another competitive outlet to fill that void.

I liked setting lofty goals and working hard to achieve them.

I continued to work out and stay in shape. I loved going to the gym.

I also had to stay in shape for my job as a police officer.

I was always looking for a way to challenge myself and I found the perfect way to do that when I started training in Jiu Jitsu.

Jiu Jitsu is a martial art and combat sport system that focuses on grappling with particular emphasis on ground fighting.

There were some similarities between Jiu Jitsu and wrestling, and that definitely benefited me when I starting training in a new sport.

I immediately developed a love and a passion for Jiu Jitsu.

In Jiu Jitsu, the athletes wear robes called Gis when they compete.

The sport is hugely popular in Japan and Brazil.

I started training in Jiu Jitsu when I was in the Police Academy in 2008.

I was lucky because my brother, William, is also a black belt in Jiu Jitsu. William told me about a great coach in Colorado Springs. Professor Lee Douglas taught me most of what I know in Jiu Jitsu and he is an amazing athlete himself. I started training with him because of how good he was and I was able to learn the sport quickly.

BELIEVE AND ACHIEVE

I was training a lot in Jiu Jitsu. It was my main hobby. I was working the midnight shift as a cop so I would have time to train in Jiu Jitsu during the day.

I worked my way up and I eventually earned a black belt in 2012.

I was never planning to compete in Jiu Jitsu, but a friend of mine asked me why I didn't compete.

I was preaching to students I worked with about competing, but I wasn't competing.

I decided to enter a Jiu Jitsu competition in a Gi in 2013 and it didn't go well. I lost my first match. My opponent didn't attempt any offensive moves, but he was awarded the victory. The decision was a little questionable, but I obviously had room for improvement.

I decided I wanted to compete again. I always wanted a chance to avenge a loss.

I went to the World Championships for No Gi Jiu Jitsu the following year. I worked my butt off.

No Gi Jiu Jitsu is like grappling. You wear MMA shorts, but not the Gi.

Going into that tournament, I felt confident I could do well. I didn't think anybody could take me down.

I won the 2014 No Gi Master World Championships in Jiu Jitsu.

The event was held in Irvine, California, about a two-hour drive down the coast from where I grew up in Lancaster.

I had to win five matches at the No Gi Worlds to win the championship. It was only my second tournament in that martial art, but I had trained in Jiu Jitsu for a number of years.

It was interesting that some of my opponents tried to take me down. They didn't know my background in wrestling.

After the fact, everyone knew that I had wrestled in the Olympics.

It was awesome when I won that title. It was a huge rush to win that tournament and stand atop the medal podium after winning a gold medal.

It felt so great to compete again. It had been six years since I had competed in a big tournament.

Jiu Jitsu became my passion after I finished my wrestling career.

It's fun for me. I'm not quite as serious about it as I was with wrestling, but I have trained extensively in Jiu Jitsu.

I was extremely excited to do something like that in a different sport from wrestling. I worked really hard for that tournament and it paid off for me.

I won a tough semifinal bout and then I faced a veteran competitor in the finals.

Paulo Pinto was very well-known. He was a Brazilian, but I had an edge on him. I was bigger and stronger, and I could really feel that when we met in the finals.

After I won, people were coming up to me and saying, "Do you realize who you just beat?"

Paulo was highly regarded in the Jiu Jitsu world.

We were in the Absolute division and anybody from any weight class could enter.

It was an enjoyable experience. And winning is always fun, so it was awesome to be on top again.

The next year, I went back for the No Gi Worlds to defend my title. But I didn't place. I lost to a strong competitor named Mahamed Aly, a Brazilian who was named after famous American boxer Muhammad Ali.

Mahamed Aly went on to win a world title in Jiu Jitsu.

He was on the cover of the magazine they handed out at the tournament, so he obviously was pretty good.

I probably didn't take my preparation for the No Gi Worlds quite as seriously as I did the year before. It's challenging when you have a job and a family and other obligations that occupy your time.

I have been a black belt for seven years so I am now a second-degree black belt in Jiu Jitsu.

After I lost at the No Gi Worlds in 2015, I started thinking like I did during my wrestling career. I sat in the stands and thought about how I needed to improve so I could beat that guy the next time I faced him. I had all of these things running through my mind that I needed to work on.

Then after a short time, reality set in. I started to think about everything else I had going on in my life. I just didn't have the time to commit to that.

Unlike my wrestling days, I had other responsibilities that took priority.

I still train in Jiu Jitsu, but definitely as more of a hobby. I love the sport, but it is nowhere near as tough as wrestling at the highest level.

My career in law enforcement definitely kept me busy.

After I joined the Colorado Springs SWAT team in 2013, I thought it was the coolest job in the world.

I had a boss, Ron Sheppard, who was awesome. He is one of the best people I know. He was very well respected.

Ron was so smart tactically. He was literally five steps ahead of everyone else. He had been a SWAT team member before he became the head of the entire team. He could be a best friend and be making jokes with you. But when it was time to be serious, he knew how to flip the switch where everybody respected him. He was a true leader.

It was a lot of fun working for the SWAT team. There was a ton of adrenaline flowing when I would go on calls.

I had found what I wanted to do forever.

I knew I was meant to do public service and now I was in a position very few people could get to.

We did a lot of search warrants for narcotics. And a lot of apprehensions of dangerous felons. We arrested people buying drugs from undercover detectives.

We trained for a number of scenarios that included hostage rescue and active shooter situations.

Training was a big part of the SWAT team. It was important to follow our tactical and strategical plan while following the proper protocol.

We were the elite group of police for making arrests, so we had to train and shoot more than everybody else.

It was a very lucky position for me to be in, but it also was a challenging and scary position.

And I was about to find that out first-hand.

CHAPTER 7
Planned Parenthood

November 27, 2015, is a day that I will never forget. It was the day after Thanksgiving. It was Black Friday, the busiest shopping day of the year, and I had a day off from the SWAT team. But as always, I was on call 24/7 and needed to be ready at any time.

Marley and I decided to take our two sons, Jameson and Cal, swimming at the indoor pool at Villa Sport, a fitness club we belonged to in northern Colorado Springs.

We were inside the pool area enjoying time with our family. I was sitting down near the pool when my cell phone rang late that morning.

My partner, Andy, was calling.

"Did you receive an alert from our dispatcher?" he said matter-of-factly.

"No, I did not," I said.

"Hey, there's an active shooter," he said. "We're getting called out."

The alert came through on my phone a short time later, but I was already on the move.

My family and I had driven together that day, so I had to get my boys out of the pool as fast as possible. I felt bad for ruining our family day and I initially was upset about the situation. But I knew what I had signed up to do and my family understood.

We were responding to a report of an active shooter inside the

BELIEVE AND ACHIEVE

Planned Parenthood clinic in Colorado Springs at 11:38 a.m. Staff inside the clinic said they heard gunfire outside and then moved people out of a waiting room and locked a security door.

As responding officers approached the building, the suspect fired at them and police returned fire before a long standoff ensued.

Initial reports described the gunman as being armed with a long gun and wearing hunting gear. Authorities later identified the weapon as a high-powered, semi-automatic rifle.

As many as 20 gunshots were fired within five minutes. Police swarmed the area, and nearby stores were put on lockdown.

I had to try and make it there as quickly and efficiently as possible, but the weather that day was horrible. It was snowing and the roads were slick from the ice that covered them. It was a nasty, freezing cold day.

Before I could go anywhere, I had to take my family home.

We lived about two miles from the gym and I obviously wanted to hurry home, but I also had to be safe because my wife and my kids were riding in the vehicle with me.

I made it home and immediately turned on my radio so I could begin gathering information.

The first thing I heard on the radio was that one of my teammates, a senior member of our team, had pulled up directly in front of the building. I could hear him screaming on the radio. He was hysterical and you could hear the fear in his voice.

He had been shot. I realized that this was an intense situation and I needed to get there as fast as possible.

I quickly changed into my SWAT team uniform, which was staged by my vehicle at all times so I could be as efficient as possible.

I jumped in my work vehicle, a Ford Expedition, and turned on my flashing lights and siren as I pulled out of my driveway.

My heart was pounding and my adrenaline was pumping as I flew out of my neighborhood.

The first turn I took, my vehicle slid sideways on the ice and I almost crashed into a curb. I told myself I better slow down or I wouldn't make it there. I had to be more careful.

My drive was across town, on the west side of Colorado Springs toward the Rocky Mountains and the Garden of the Gods.

All I was heard on the radio was chaos and I was trying to decipher what was going on. I needed to figure out what they were going to need from me when I arrived.

We had done extensive amounts of active shooter training and we had certain protocol that we followed.

A short time later, I heard on the radio that another police officer had been shot. And from the way it sounded, he may have died.

It took me 20 minutes to arrive at the scene, so a lot had happened before I even showed up.

SWAT has the most training and experience, but we aren't typically the first officers to respond.

When I first arrived to join my team, we were about a quarter-mile north of the building where the shootings took place. I climbed into an armored vehicle, we met the rest of our team and the team was given a quick debrief of what was happening.

At the time, we didn't know how many shooters there were. It was still pretty chaotic.

There was no time to waste and our boss provided us with instructions.

"Hey, we're going to go in. This guy has already shot several people. He has killed several people, including a cop. We need to get in there."

My heart was racing and the adrenaline was pumping once again. This situation was very real and it was what we had trained for.

Reality set in quickly, to say the least.

Our team loaded up into one of the armed vehicles and I could see the serious look on everyone's faces.

It was a difficult situation, but I was with an elite group of people and there was nobody I trusted more. Our team was known to be one of the best in the area and we took great pride in our jobs.

It was a day none of us would ever forget.

We headed down to Planned Parenthood in one armored vehicle. There were around a dozen people in the vehicle – SWAT team members, K9 officers and medical personnel.

We had another vehicle that went around the front of the building to try and distract the shooter while we approached the building from the back.

As we approached the building, we threw smoke grenades to lower the visibility of our team.

On our way to the building, the officer who had been killed was still on the ground and within sight of us.

As I exited the vehicle, I said a prayer silently to myself.

Please watch over our team. And if something happens to any of us, please watch over our families.

This was a pressure-packed situation.

Being an Olympic-level athlete had taught me to perform under stress and I believe that carried over into my career in law enforcement.

This obviously wasn't the same – it was much more serious – but it was a stressful situation and we were tasked with stopping the threat. And I had been in situations as an athlete where I had to perform under pressure.

This was a time where I was legitimately scared, but I had a job to do. I had to maintain my focus and keep my composure.

Right away, we entered the building and started moving tactically through. Within a very short time, I made one of the biggest mistakes of my career as did a couple of my teammates.

My partner and I moved into a room and then two other SWAT officers pushed through an original room they cleared and came into our room from an opposite door. They didn't realize we were there already.

We were each armed with an MP7, a compact, lightweight defense weapon that could be carried like a handgun but had rifle-like effectiveness.

Once we entered the dark room, we could only see reflections of each other.

When my teammates entered the room from the opposite side, I saw a silhouette with someone pointing a gun at me. I believe they saw the same thing and unfortunately, we fired at each other.

One bullet went whizzing right by us, just missing us by inches, as they started firing multiple rounds into the room.

When I fired, I unfortunately hit my target as I was trained to do. But as soon as I pulled the trigger, I realized I had shot one of my teammates.

The bullet hit center mass, where his hand was and ricocheted into his left shoulder area.

As they continued to fire, I yelled multiple times, "Cease fire, blue on blue" until the bullets stopped.

A couple of my teammates pulled the person who had been shot outside and I saw blood on the ground. I knew who I had hit because I heard him screaming as he fired his weapon at where he believed there was a threat.

I quickly grabbed another member of our team while trying to catch my breath.

"Please tell me it hit his vest," I said.

"No, man, I don't think it did," he said, shaking his head.

That obviously wasn't the response I wanted to hear, and that scared the hell out of me.

But that is all we knew at the time.

And I wouldn't have any news on my teammate for the next several hours.

All of our shooting happened within the first minute after we entered the clinic.

One of the senior guys on the team actually walked up to me with a concerned look on his face.

"Hey, I'm going to take you out of here," he said.

"No, I'm fine," I responded.

He didn't know my emotional state after that happened, but I wasn't going to quit on my team. I wasn't going anywhere.

I was able to regain my focus shortly after and continue the job we were there to do. But in the back of my head, I worried about my teammate for the next several hours.

Our focus was trying to help civilians safely make it out of the building.

Shortly after, I heard an exchange of gunfire from a loud rifle. That was the rifle used by the gunman we were trying to locate.

BELIEVE AND ACHIEVE

We didn't know exactly where he was and it took us a while to pin down his location.

Over the next few hours, the suspect was shooting through random walls and the rounds from his weapon were literally flying by SWAT team members' heads.

Hundreds of rounds were shot inside that building.

It was a very, very scary situation. I saw multiple SWAT officers get shot literally a few feet away from my location.

We had to be very cautious because there were multiple civilians involved and we were there to protect them. We didn't want to put them in more danger.

Eventually, we were able to figure out where the suspect was and establish containment around his location.

Part of our team held containment on the shooter and the rest of us went around the building to start evacuating people.

We were in there for what seemed like an eternity. It was nerve-wracking and it was emotional.

After a standoff that lasted more than five hours, our teams crashed armored vehicles into the lobby.

The aggressive tactics worked.

The attacker eventually surrendered at 4:52 p.m.

Robert Lewis Dear Jr. was taken into custody and charged with first-degree murder and ordered held without bond.

Finally, it was over, but this was an event that will live with us for the rest of our lives.

Everybody on our team was really down when the ordeal ended. It was devastating.

It was an unbelievable and unforgettable day. It was so tragic and took a huge toll on us.

A short time later, while we were still inside the building, one of the sergeants in the police department approached me with news I had been anxiously waiting to hear.

"He's going to be OK," the sergeant said.

"Thank God," I responded.

The sergeant was talking about the teammate that I had accidentally shot.

Overcoming Obstacles to Excel

I breathed a huge sigh of relief. I had been very concerned about him during the entire five hours we were inside the building.

I was so grateful that he was going to be all right. A huge weight had been lifted off my chest.

Three other SWAT team members had been shot at the scene. Two were in surgery and the third was OK.

The enormity of the tragic day really hit me at that point. It was overwhelming.

It was a very emotional moment, and I broke down and began to cry.

I had an incredible level of respect for the people on the SWAT team and for all of the police officers who responded that day.

All of these people have families and they all put their lives on the line to save the civilians in the clinic.

There were mistakes made, including a huge one I made, but every single cop that went in there risked their own life. I blame no one for their mistakes and own up to my own.

There is nothing more admirable and honorable than the brave people who went in there that day to try and help others.

In my eyes, they are all heroes.

The mass shooting that day resulted in the deaths of three people and injuries to nine. A police officer and two civilians were killed; five police officers and four civilians were injured.

The story became national news and dominated television broadcasts on CNN, NBC, ABC and CBS.

It was a horrific ordeal, but it could have been much worse.

From the moment the first police officer arrived, no more civilians were injured. That was a win in my book and the reason we all did what we did.

The standoff was over, but we weren't allowed to go home and see our families right away.

At that time, all I wanted to do was see my family and let them know how much I loved them.

I am not a guy who cries a lot, but I was an emotional wreck that day. Everybody on our team had the same feelings.

It took months after the incident to complete the investigation as to what exactly had happened.

They interviewed me that night about what happened when members of our team accidentally shot at each other.

I also found the teammate who had been shot. We had shot at each other, but we hugged and apologized to each other. We were just doing what we were trained to do in the worst situation of our careers.

We weren't the first ones on our SWAT team that had done that in a high-risk situation.

You try your best to train to avoid it, but you can't.

Unfortunately, I learned that guys who made the same mistake in the past were too proud, or maybe ashamed. And no one stepped up to use their experience to help me dealing with mine.

It took me a long time to get over that mistake, but I owned up to it from the beginning.

I believe you need to own the mistakes and move on.

I will never deny the fact that I made a mistake.

I moved on and hopefully our team would learn from it in the future.

It was a hugely traumatic experience.

Some people dealt with it well and some people on our team were having trouble coping.

One of my best friends, Tim, was on the SWAT team with me, but a K9 officer at the time of the incident.

We talked about what happened and I think it enabled us to deal with what had transpired.

We continued conversations about it for the next few years and I know it helped me a lot.

Our wives actually watched the standoff unfold on television that day. Obviously, I know it was really stressful for them when they were sitting there watching while their husbands were there at the scene.

The best way for me to cope was to talk about it. That helped me as I tried to move forward with my life and my career.

The department had us talk to the police psychologist, but quite frankly it didn't help me.

I think it was more for them to say they tried to help than anything else.

I know there was some post-traumatic stress with a lot of people and that was definitely understandable.

We spent a couple of hours after the standoff doing interviews at our offices and talking about everything that had happened.

They were still trying to put all of the pieces together.

We were finally allowed to go home to our families that evening.

I had called Marley immediately after the suspect was arrested and let her know I was OK.

I can't imagine what she was going through in the time before I was able to finally call her. I'm sure it was a helpless feeling for those five long hours we were in that clinic.

When I arrived home and saw my family, it really hit home how serious the situation I was in that day.

If one bullet had flown a different direction, I wouldn't have seen them again.

I may not have gone home that day to my wife and my kids.

I was really emotional when I got home.

I hugged Marley, and I hugged my kids.

"I love you guys," I said with tears welling in my eyes.

"I love you, too," Marley said, while pulling me close in an embrace.

It was a very stressful time for us and it was a huge relief to be home with my family.

I knew there were three people who were shot and killed that day who weren't going home to see their families.

It was heartbreaking to think about.

I couldn't imagine what their families were going through.

I felt very fortunate. I had survived the scariest day of my life.

And it was another reminder of how dangerous what I was doing for a living.

Around 11 months later, I was notified that I was being honored for my role at the clinic on the day of the shootings.

I had earned the medal of honor.

All of our SWAT team members involved that day were chosen to receive that prestigious honor.

The medal of honor is considered the highest honor you can

receive in the police department.

I had mixed emotions about the whole thing. It was a very trying ordeal at the clinic and it wasn't really something you felt good about.

I beat myself up about what happened, but over time I gained more of an appreciation for being honored.

I initially told Marley that I would not accept the award because it was not deserved. After several conversations with friends and other members of the team, including some high-ranking past team members, I realized that many of us made mistakes.

But it took me a while to accept that.

The SWAT team played an important role in defusing a situation that could have turned out even worse.

That day used to be on my mind every day, but over time I didn't think about it as much.

Shortly after that incident, I received a page about a shooter with a rifle. My heart started pounding again and I started thinking about that day at the clinic.

Sometimes, when I hear loud noises that sound like gunshots, it startles me more than it would a lot of people. Fireworks make me jumpy after the experience I went through. I usually play it off like I am just joking around.

It is all becoming a memory now and not so much something that bothers me anymore.

Those medals are cool, but it represents the worst day of my life other than family members dying.

I was never doing that job to earn a medal.

I'm happy that they recognized our team for our efforts. The team did great work that day.

I was there to do a job and it was a rough day.

It was the worst day of my professional career. It was awful seeing people lose their lives that day.

We were just grateful that we were able to help some people out of a horrible situation.

Being a member of the SWAT team was really, really cool to me for about two years. But the novelty was starting to wear off. It began to wear on me because we had young kids and I was on call 24/7.

Overcoming Obstacles to Excel

Prior to the Planned Parenthood incident, I started looking at other jobs in the police department and I also started talking to a buddy about becoming a firefighter.

I also knew some former wrestlers involved with medical sales and I was looking into that as well. I had always worked in public service, but I was considering doing something else.

I realized that I wasn't satisfied with what I was doing anymore. The schedule was a challenge for me and we worked some crazy hours.

The SWAT team just wasn't a good fit for me anymore.

I needed to make a change. Some people think I left because of the Planned Parenthood incident, but that was not the case.

A couple of months before the Planned Parenthood incident, I had contacted the Denver Fire Department about the possibility of working for them.

And I was about to make another career move.

CHAPTER 8
Becoming a Firefighter

I left the Colorado Springs Police Department and joined the Denver Fire Department in 2016. And I'm so glad that I did. This job is more satisfying for me and it's just a better fit for me.

I still work in public service and I really enjoy what I'm doing.

I applied for a job in the fire department in the fall of 2015 while I was still working for the SWAT team in the Springs.

I had done my research before I filled out an interest form with the fire department.

I knew some people who worked in the fire department and I tried to gather information about the job from them. I wanted to be ready if they contacted me.

The next step was to take a written test late in 2015.

I received a score of 98.6 percent on test and scored high enough to move on to the next step.

I had to take a fitness test.

I had to wear a 70-pound vest and walk on a Stairmaster for several minutes.

I had to go through a dark tunnel, and then after that pick up and carry equipment. And I had to raise a ladder.

It was a close simulation to some of the duties I would have as a firefighter.

It was a fairly basic test and it was pretty easy, especially after being on the SWAT team.

After the fitness test, I underwent psychological testing.

I took a polygraph test and underwent a psychological interview.

They wanted to make sure I was being truthful with our resume and information, and wanted to make sure I didn't have a criminal history.

I took a drug test and then they did a background interview that included previous jobs and references.

A lot of paperwork was involved.

It was a time-consuming process, but it was more than worth it.

There were so many different steps involved as the fire department ran through their pool of candidates.

It's a very competitive job. And it's not easy to land a position there.

When I applied, there was a limit on the number of people who would could apply.

The process took about a year.

A buddy of mine who was a firefighter in Colorado Springs told me I should apply in Denver because the hours and pay were better.

It turned out to be a great recommendation.

I was offered a position with the Denver Fire Department in August of 2016. I started in the Fire Academy on September 6.

I was very fortunate that I was hired that quickly.

I had also been looking into going into medical sales. I likely would have gone that route if I hadn't been hired by the fire department.

I was ready to do something different. The job satisfaction with the SWAT team was completely gone.

I wasn't disgruntled, but I wasn't happy either. I didn't want to stay in a job where I might be complaining.

It didn't have anything to do with the danger element of my job with the SWAT team. Or anything to do with the experiences I had with the police department.

Part of me wanted to stay with the SWAT team because of my teammates. It was harder for me to leave after the Planned Parenthood incident and it was an emotional time.

We had built a great camaraderie on our team after that incident. We had a close-knit group on the SWAT team.

It was bittersweet when I left the police department, but I was excited to join the fire department.

Once I talked with Marley and made the decision to make the move, I was 100 percent sure it was the right decision.

Being a cop wore on me and I decided it wasn't the best career path anymore.

I admire the people in that profession. I have the utmost respect for them. Police officers have the toughest job out there and there is a lot of negative sentiment toward them from the public.

The chief of police in Colorado Springs signed a letter telling me I was welcome to come back to the department within a year if things didn't work out with the fire department.

It was something that was pretty common for them to do, but it was still nice.

I had something to fall back on and it was a safety net if the fire department wasn't a good fit.

The next step was to enter the Fire Academy in Denver.

It was a four-month process and it wasn't easy.

The days were long. I had no knowledge of being a firefighter and I was very naïve to the firefighting world.

My work week would start early, long before the sun came up.

I would leave my house in Colorado Springs at 3 a.m. every Monday and then arrive a little over an hour later in Denver.

It was a 75-mile drive.

In the beginning, there were days I was still at the Fire Academy until 7 or 8 o'clock at night.

After I got home, I would study before bed.

During my time at the Fire Academy, my mother-in-law Mamie offered me a place to stay during the week so I didn't have to drive back-and-forth between Colorado Springs and Denver. She lived 10 minutes away from the academy.

There was no way I could've commuted during the week with my crazy schedule.

It would've been too exhausting. I was tired enough when I was staying in Denver.

I really appreciated my mother-in-law for doing that. We didn't see each other a lot, but we would go out to dinner once a week.

BELIEVE AND ACHIEVE

Those dinners were nice because we would talk and take the focus off the academy. My brother-in-law, Stephen, and my wife's cousin, Hilary, would sometimes join us.

When I was at the academy, the schedule was pretty rough on my family. Marley was working full-time and we had two young boys at home. She started her day by taking one son to day care and our other son to school. And then she would drive to work.

She would have to pick up the kids after school and then they also had activities.

The academy was 100 percent harder on my wife than it was for me. She was the only one with the kids during the week when I was at the academy.

I would go home to Colorado Springs on the weekends, but I would still have to study a few hours a day.

It was a very challenging time, and it was really tough on my wife.

I appreciate her so much for all of the sacrifices that she made.

I took a huge pay cut when I switched jobs. My annual salary dropped $35,000 when I joined the fire department.

I was making close to $90,000 a year when I worked for the SWAT team.

And now, with the pay increases I've received over the past few years, I'm actually making more than that with the fire department.

I love my job, but there are challenging components.

Firefighters work a crazy schedule, but my schedule works really well with my kids being involved in so many activities.

We bought a house in Monument, and it's a great location for us. Marley has a short commute south to work in Colorado Springs. And I have a little bit longer commute north to Denver, but I don't have to make as many trips as she does.

I work a 24-hour shift with the fire department and then have the next 48 hours off.

It was an adjustment going to that schedule, but I love it.

It's worked out really well for me and my family.

I work every third Saturday, and that's caused me to miss a few of my kids' activities.

Overcoming Obstacles to Excel

The good part is I am able to spend much more time with them than I did when I was with the SWAT team. And I am off two out of every three Saturdays.

It's not ideal, but it's pretty good for the most part.

My wife has been incredibly supportive. Marley continues to teach social studies at Jenkins Middle School in Colorado Springs, where she's been employed for 13 years. She earned her master's degree and has been successful in her career.

She is a hard worker and is very passionate about what she does.

I'm biased, of course, but I'm really proud of her and what she's accomplished.

She also is an amazing mother to our two boys. Jameson is 9 years old and Macallan is 7.

Jameson is already excelling in baseball and wrestling. He is taking after his dad as one of the bigger kids in his class. He was already wrestling in the 95-pound class at age 9. Baseball and wrestling are his favorite sports. He likes the New York Yankees.

Jameson wants to play every sport. For his age, he does exceptionally well in baseball. He plays first base, third base, catcher and pitcher. He hits with some power, and he led his team with a number of batting stats.

Jameson has really progressed in wrestling. He has a great attitude about wrestling some older kids and he wants to become better.

It was a proud moment for our family when Jameson won a Colorado age-group state title in 2019. The best part was seeing the smile on his face. He truly is enjoying wrestling and that is a bond we share with a mutual love for the sport.

My younger son, Cal, is very active and he enjoys playing a number of sports. He has tried wrestling and he also likes playing basketball and soccer. He really likes basketball and he was part of a team that had a successful season on the court. He is a fan of the Denver Nuggets and enjoys going to their NBA games at the Pepsi Center in Denver.

Cal also likes riding his skateboard and making videos of it in our neighborhood. He's a sweet, fun-loving kid.

My sons get along really well. They fight and bicker over little things like brothers that close in age typically do. I understand what it's like to have a brother that is close in age.

I'm extremely proud of my boys and I'm looking forward to seeing them grow and develop.

I am hoping to attend the U.S. Olympic Trials for wrestling in 2020. I haven't been back to that event since I qualified for the Olympics in 2008.

I would definitely like to go again.

The Olympic Trials certainly provided me with one of the highlights of my wrestling career.

I'm still a big fan of wrestling and I follow the sport. There are guys that I used to train with, like 2016 Olympian Robby Smith, who are still competing.

I would've loved to have gone to the Olympic Trials in 2012 and 2016 to watch. But I was busy with my family and my career.

2020 would be a perfect time to reunite with people I knew from my wrestling days. I also would like to expose my sons to it and give them an opportunity to witness it.

You can't beat the competition at the Olympic Trials. The stakes are so high and the matches mean so much.

I trained for eight years on the Senior level before I made an Olympic Team in 2008.

I don't train like that anymore, but I maintain an active lifestyle. I work out at least once a day.

I lift weights and I also continue to train in Jiu Jitsu.

I also have appeared in Men's Health magazine and was named one of Men's Health top five Ultimate Guys in 2015.

I grew up reading a lot of the health and bodybuilding magazines, and I did a lot of the workouts from those publications to try and get better.

I started buying many of the magazines when I was an overweight high school freshman who wanted to get into shape so I could improve as a wrestler.

I never dreamed or imagined I would end up on the cover of Men's Health, so it was pretty awesome when it happened.

The Men's Health cover I was on went out nationwide and that opened the door for another opportunity.

I was offered a chance to be an Isopure model in 2016. I appeared in a promotional video that they used. In one of the commercials, you can see the tattoo on the upper part of my left arm that says "Beijing 2008" and has the Olympic rings below it.

In the Isopure ad, I delivered this message:

"The purest moment of my athletic career is 100 percent the Olympics. Even though I didn't win, I was still on that podium representing my country for the sport I put so many hours into. That feeling is indescribable."

The Isopure ad ended up in virtually every major men's magazine, including GQ, Men's Health, Men's Fitness and Flex.

Isopure manufactures a line of high-protein supplements marketed to body builders or those trying to lose weight and gain muscle mass.

Another bonus from that was that I received free Isopure products for three years.

I also recently released a DVD in which I show moves and techniques for Jiu Jitsu and wrestling.

Sales of the DVD have gone well and I was excited to share some of my knowledge in the video. It was enjoyable to have that opportunity.

I still love to challenge myself physically and mentally.

Between the summer of 2017 and the summer of 2018, I did a triathlon, a powerlifting competition, two cross-fit competitions and competed in two different Jiu Jitsu matches.

As the calendar flipped to 2019, I was debating on whether to do another triathlon or enter a bodybuilding competition.

It's important in my job to be physically fit, so staying active and training for competitions helps me to do that.

Going to the gym is part of my daily routine and I really enjoy it.

It is my time to unwind and have to myself.

And I like to push myself. I've always worked hard.

I love the feeling of completing a workout and the satisfaction that goes with it.

Through my life and my experiences, I really developed a strong work ethic. Not just in sports, but also with my career and with my everyday life.

I entered the Gi World Championships in California in 2018 and my first match was against a Brazilian they call "Cyborg." He's a full-time Jiu Jitsu athlete, where for me it is a hobby.

The guy's name is Roberto Abreu.

He's probably the most accomplished guy I've ever done Jiu Jitsu with.

And I almost beat him.

We were tied with 15 seconds left before he caught me in a triangle choke to beat me.

He executed a move from a position where I thought I was going to score.

I still think I can beat him. I want a rematch.

That's my mentality from my wrestling days.

I always want a chance to bounce back after a loss. And I may go back there to try and avenge that defeat.

I don't consider myself an athlete like I did during my wrestling days, so it's obviously not my priority. But I still don't like to lose.

It's been more than a decade since I wrestled in the Olympic Games, but I still enjoy competing.

I also love the process of setting a goal and then embarking on a journey to achieve it.

There is nothing quite like working hard and then accomplishing something you've set your mind to.

Developing a strong mindset helped pave the way for me to reach many of the goals that I set out to achieve in athletics and in my career.

Very few people believed I was going to make the 2008 Olympic Team, but I believed that I could.

Virtually nobody gave me a chance to medal at the Olympics either, but that didn't stop me from landing a spot on the medal podium in Beijing.

A decade after wrestling in the Olympic Games, I received one of the highest honors of my career.

I was inducted into the California Wrestling Hall of Fame in 2018.

Overcoming Obstacles to Excel

2008 Olympian Marcie Van Dusen also was in that hall of fame class with me. Marcie had excelled in women's freestyle wrestling. She was one of only three people to defeat Japan's Saori Yoshida, who won 13 World titles and three Olympic gold medals.

There have been so many outstanding wrestlers that have come out of California, including 1984 Olympic gold medalists Dave and Mark Schultz, and 2012 Olympic champion Jake Varner.

Stephen Neal was a wrestler from California that I really looked up to when I was growing up. He won two NCAA titles for Cal State Bakersfield and captured a World title in freestyle wrestling before going on to excel in the National Football League. Neal won three Super Bowl rings as an offensive lineman for the New England Patriots.

I always thought if I wrestled in college that I wanted to go to Cal State Bakersfield and wrestle like Stephen Neal.

It was a great honor and privilege for me to join the hall of fame in my home state.

It was awesome to share that night with people that are close to me. I had 42 family and friends that attended the hall of fame ceremony.

My wife was there along with my mother, my father and my brother and sister.

My mother, Julie, was the person who was there for everything from Day 1. Her support meant more than me than winning an Olympic medal. She's battled her own demons, but she did a great job raising us under difficult circumstances. No matter how poor we were or how tough things were, she was always there for all three of her kids.

And of course, my wife has been incredibly supportive. Marley is the love of my life. She's an amazing woman and I am so blessed that she came into my life. She was really there for me during some challenging times I've encountered as an athlete and in my professional career in public service. I'm so glad she still let me talk to her after I deleted her AOL message when we were in college. I'm a lucky guy to have her as my partner on this crazy journey.

It meant a great deal to have my family and friends there when I

BELIEVE AND ACHIEVE

was inducted into the California Wrestling Hall of Fame on May 5, 2018, in Laguna Hills, California.

This is the speech that I delivered the night I was inducted.

First of all, I want to start off by saying thank you for including me in this year's induction into the California Wrestling Hall of Fame. It's an honor to be included into this prestigious group of individuals. Also, congratulations to all the other 2018 inductees. You all deserve it very much and I am happy to be able to share this evening with you.

For those who have known me since I started wrestling, we all know I would probably be voted least likely to succeed in wrestling. I started as a freshman and literally had no idea what I was getting myself into. I still remember the first practice where I couldn't complete anything the coaches asked us to do. So along with being horribly weak and out of shape, I also didn't know how to wrestle. I was by far the worst guy on my team and finished the season 1-15.

After my freshman year of wrestling, I had some internal drive to become better. I hated that I was not succeeding. I started working out, lifting weights, and doing everything I could to become stronger and better prepared for the following season. Often times, I would "practice" my moves on my brother and sister on the living room floor.

Even though I was focusing on becoming better at the sport of wrestling, my grades were slipping. I was hanging out with the wrong crowd and eventually dropped out of high school in an attempt to go to a continuation school.

Luckily for me, I mentioned leaving school to Coach Eisel, and he decided to step in and become the most impactful person in my wrestling career. Coach Eisel took me under his wing and started making me work out with him in the offseason. He showed me what hard work was all about. He started taking me to church, and became a mentor to me in all aspects of life. Coach Eisel also was able to get me back into school at the start of my junior year.

Coach Eisel taught me not only about physical strength, but mental strength as well. One example I would like to note is the time where he almost killed us on a 25-mile hike in the middle of the summer in the desert of California. But don't worry, Coach, I don't hold grudges.

Overcoming Obstacles to Excel

After getting back into school, I was very fortunate to not only have Coach Eisel by my side but I also gained two coaches who eventually became like older brothers to me. Mike Henery and Steve Radford started helping my wrestling team and were two guys that I looked up to very much. Both of them are like big brothers to me. Of course, in this case the little brother is the toughest.

My junior and senior year in high school, I continued to get better at wrestling and also focused on school. I did have a good senior year record of 44-3, however, I lost my first match of the Masters meet and never even qualified for the state tournament.

Even though my high school wrestling career was over without a state championship, I still accomplished huge things with the work ethic instilled in me by my three coaches and by my mother. I also was able to graduate high school with my original class.

After high school, I joined the military. And shortly after that, I was introduced to the Navy wrestling team, which would be my team for the next five years. I definitely believe you are a product of your environment and I was thrust into an environment where I was bound to succeed if I was willing to put in the work.

My first year on the Navy team, my coach was the head Olympic coach for the Greco-Roman wrestling team, Rob Hermann. And one of my teammates, Steve Mays, made the Olympic Team that year. Being put into that environment, with coaches and athletes around me like that, made me realize what is possible with hard work.

Going straight from high school to the Senior level of wrestling was a huge step. The following two years I won a total of one match and the ones I lost were usually by tech fall or pin. I was very far behind the competition.

Even though I was not performing well at the Olympic level, I still continued to work hard and enjoy the process of getting better. Which eventually happened. After a couple of years on the Navy team, I was fortunate again to get a teammate who became another mentor, Neal Rodak. I was lucky enough to have a dorm room right next to Neal's. At the time, Neal was the best wrestler on the Navy team. Unlike myself, Neal started at such a high level after high school and he was an NCAA All-American. I was lucky enough to see how hard

BELIEVE AND ACHIEVE

he worked, which showed me that if I wanted to be successful, I would have to work that hard, too. Neal was in my corner at the Olympic Trials and I couldn't have asked for anyone better.

In 2002, 2003 and 2004, I won silver medals in the Armed Forces Wrestling Championships. In 2004, I was fourth at the Olympic Trials where I beat past World Team members and other high-level wrestlers. That gave me the confidence to believe that I could make the Olympic Team in 2008.

The following year in 2005, I finished second in the country behind a guy who continued to beat me every year until 2008. Never once was I the No. 1 guy in the country or would have been anyone's top choice to make the 2008 Olympic Team.

From 2004 to 2008, I competed in over 25 countries and some of them multiple times. I also competed in all of the tournaments held in the United States to try and prepare myself to make the 2008 Olympic Team. During that time, I trained at the Olympic Training Center and my confidence grew and I started to believe that I could actually do it. I believed I was the hardest-working guy in the room during my final few years.

Just when I thought my preparation was going as good as it could, I lost my first match at the 2008 U.S. Nationals to a guy who I had never lost to before. This was only two months before the Olympic Trials. This was a time with support from my coaches, family and especially my wife, Marley, I was able to get through and still believe in myself for the Olympic Trials. I continued to work harder than I had ever worked before and lucky for me I made the Olympic Team and was able to bring home a bronze medal for my country.

I definitely don't believe that any of this would have been possible without the support of my family, friends, coaches, and my wife, Marley. I would like to thank all my family and friends who supported me during my career and who are here with me today. This includes Carol Raanes, Uncle John, and Aunt Diana, who are watching from above. You guys all being there for me means more to me than any medal I have won. I love you all and again thank you.

It was an amazing night at the hall of fame ceremony.

It's been quite a journey. My story is one of perseverance and one of overcoming obstacles to excel.

No matter where you come from, you can still accomplish great things in your life.

If you believe it, you can achieve it.

I achieved what I did through hard work, not natural talent.

I use the mental toughness I developed in wrestling in all aspects of my life.

If you work hard, believe in yourself and develop the right mindset, anything is possible.

I know it was for me.